RATIONAL
BEHAVIOR
An Explanation
of Behavior That Is Especially
Human

BY MYLES I. FRIEDMAN

The book describes a psychological theory of rational behavior. The theory posits that the primary force directing behavior is the individual's inherent motivation to predict his relationship with the environment. Mental process and behavior, then, are organized to confirm predictions. The individual is behaving rationally when he makes predictions and attempts to confirm them.

Psychological theories often emphasize man's commonalities with lower creatures. Consequently, they slight rationality. Professor Friedman's systematic explanation of rationality focuses more on human excellence. He explains how individuals discover and invent. The implications of the theory for learning, individual adjustment, and social systems highlight the contributions of this work to our understanding of human behavior.

"Professor Friedman has taken a very bold thesis in *Rational Behavior* and has explored some of the ramifications of this thesis for behavior, education, and other areas. He has created a model which strikes out in a very new direction, and it is likely to be some time before many of the social science disciplines recognize the full force of his ideas. I believe that further research by social scientists will bear out the main thesis and the supporting arguments. I am confident that the book will have major influences on research and conceptualization in various disciplines concerned with the nature of man, his *Weltanschauung,* and his social and political institutions."

RATIONAL
BEHAVIOR

RATIONAL BEHAVIOR

*An Explanation of Behavior
That Is Especially Human*

MYLES I. FRIEDMAN

UNIVERSITY OF SOUTH CAROLINA PRESS

COLUMBIA, SOUTH CAROLINA

Library of Congress Cataloging in Publication Data

Friedman, Myles I   1924–
    Rational behavior: an explanation of behavior that
is especially human.

    Bibliography: p.
    Includes index.
    1. Psychology. I. Title. [DNLM: 1. Behavior.
2. Psychological theory. BF38 F911r]
BF38.F74   153   75–2416
ISBN 0–87249–325–3

To my sister Blossom

CONTENTS

vii

ACKNOWLEDGMENTS

I wish to express my appreciation to the people who supported me and contributed toward the improvement of the book. I am especially grateful to those who served as my mentors while the book was being written—Walt Procko, Glen Martin, David Garron, and George Lackey, Jr. They read my visions and revisions and sharpened and clarified my thinking.

Benjamin Bloom, Leon Lessinger, Bruno Bettelheim, Robert Gagné, Robert Thorndike, Robert McCarder, Claude Mathis, Arthur Jensen, and Jacob Getzels were kind enough to review the first draft of the manuscript. I am indebted to them for their encouragement and for the contributions they made to improve the book.

INTRODUCTION

The accumulation of theories in the behavioral sciences obliges the proponent of any new theory to explain why it is needed. Speculation as a pastime is all very well at a social gathering or for personal amusement, but as a serious scientific pursuit it is subject to formal restraints. These include the support of a reasonable amount of objective evidence; a constructive departure from current theories; the possibility of finding out the extent to which the theory is accurate; enough simplicity, parsimony, and internal consistency so that one can understand it more easily than the things it tries to explain; and, finally, the possibility that it will provide a base from which others may expand present knowledge.

A theory that lacks such characteristics is merely idle speculation—amusing, perhaps, to its inventor but not really helpful to anyone. The world needs knowledge and clarification, not casual fancy offered as wisdom. Some psychologists maintain that although a theory might possess all the formal restraints needed to give it substance, it nevertheless restricts discovery because it biases investigation.

I shall not belabor the practicality of theory. My purpose is to place the theory proposed in this book within a general schema of behavioral theories in which it will be seen primarily as complementing rather than contradicting existing theories. To the extent that it clarifies the puzzling behavior of human beings, it may be viewed, because of its departure from other theories, as "competing" with these theories. I am more interested, however, in showing that its focus highlights certain neglected matters than in declaring war on existing interpretations of behavior.

INTRODUCTION

Any light that can be shed on behavior should be welcomed by all concerned, particularly at this early stage in the science of human behavior. If we can make behavior more approachable, more predictable, and more amenable to civilized influence, the theory offered here will be a justified addition to other theories, however numerous they may be. Indeed, there are certain shortcomings inherent in the very process of theorizing that seem to make it desirable to have several or even many theories in behavioral science. Let us examine these shortcomings.

A theory is not, of course, the reality it seeks to explain. It is a selective observation—through particular eyeglasses—from a specific vantage point. To the degree that it selects from the ceaseless flux of reality, it is less than a total account; and to be partial is to be inaccurate. The more one attends to an area of interest from a particular vantage point, the more one minimizes or distorts peripheral matters. Theoretical bias enters as soon as one defines a focus for observing reality. This is true not only because the nature of human thought prohibits one from seeing the detailed and the general with equal clarity at the same time, but also, more importantly, because a theory starts with a reference point, which in turn defines a corresponding view of the world.

In order for a theory to generate pertinent, testable hypotheses, it must focus on the phenomena of interest so that accurate observations can be made. Peripheral data will inevitably get lost or overlooked in this process. But this limitation in scope or detail is not necessarily fatal, for the focus is narrowed—or, in some cases, widened—deliberately, to observe the kind of phenomena in question. As the investigator moves closer to observe more minute phenomena, his scope narrows. As he withdraws to gain a more comprehensive view of the field, he sacrifices accuracy of detail. A study of macrocosms focuses broadly at the expense of details. A study of the neurology of individuals will give short shrift to international affairs. To theorize is to commit oneself to something less than omniscience. One can theorize only about a subset of the world's lavish data. A theory may, in a lucky case, explain somewhat more than it was originally intended to; by its very nature, however, it cannot explain everything. To insist, then,

INTRODUCTION

on viewing all the world from the vantage point of a single theory, as some have tended to do, is simply to adopt it as one's personal philosophy.

Thus, the nature of theorizing is responsible for some of the limitations found in particular theories. These characteristics of theorizing suggest that a relatively comprehensive and accurate explanation of reality would require a multitude of interlocking, interfacilitating theories, each constituting an observation post on the universe. These points of view are theoretical biases. They are the built-in risks and limitations of theorizing.

I acknowledge, then, that the behavioral theory I am proposing, like any theory, has a particular bias. This bias describes both the limitations and the promise of the theory. New biases represent new viewpoints, and new viewpoints can lead to new knowledge. The territory into which the bias of my theory takes us is infrequently explored. It is hoped that the venture will provide some pertinent leads or information.

The book is divided into three parts. Part I consists of the first two chapters. In chapter 1, I shall define the focus of a theory of rational behavior and attempt to show that this focus has been overlooked and neglected. In chapter 2 I shall give examples of various views on rationality offered by persons who are concerned with the subject, but who have not attempted to offer a formal and comprehensive account of rationality. In pointing out some of the limitations of these views, I do not intend to discredit their quality. On the contrary, these views are included here because of their significance. My purpose is merely to indicate that there is justification for probing further into the subject of rationality.

Part II consists of a formal presentation of the theory. In Part III, I deal with some of the implications of the theory. Part III begins with the direct implications of the theory (chapters 12 and 13). The theory is psychological; therefore, the direct implications are concerned primarily with the individual as an individual. Then, in the last chapters, less direct implications are considered, bearing mainly on society's influence on the individual.

PART I / BACKGROUND

1

THE THEORY: AN ORIENTATION

To elucidate the bias of my theory, I shall examine four arbitrarily chosen but perhaps representative determinants of behavior. Most existing views of behavior can be identified as emphasizing one of the following four determinants: two determinants, social and physical influences, represent forces of the environment; two others, the biological and rational, represent forces emanating from the individual. Of course, any conscientious theory of behavior and learning is likely to allude to each of these four influences. Differences among the viewpoints of various theories will tend, then, to be matters of emphasis within this framework.

In order to highlight the biases of each of these viewpoints, I shall polarize my references to them. This will result in an oversimplified and exaggerated view of each position, but such polarization will serve to present each veiwpoint in substantial contrast to the others, so that the bias of the proposed theory may be understood clearly.

One theory, for example, may stress the physical aspects of the environment. Behavior may be said to occur as a result of the physical forces of the environment. Food pellets or electric shock might constitute independent variables that change or shape behavior. Analogously, a theory may emphasize the social factors of the environment. The individual is viewed as dependent upon his society for survival; hence he conforms to its expectations. From this viewpoint, conformity may be considered the primary be-

3

havior determinant. In some contrast, an emphasis on biological factors of the individual may suggest that desire or need is the dynamic cause of behavior. Behavior then will be directed toward the satisfaction of desires; the social, physical, and rational factors will inevitably suffer corresponding neglect.

On the other hand, there are few if any theories that focus on the rational ability of the individual as the primary behavior determinant. It is not that serious theorists in the biological, social, or physical traditions ignore the rational aspect of behavior; they simply do not view it as an initiating force. In the original Freudian theory, for example, rational insight via the ego is considered a factor determining behavior. But the ego is relegated to the status of procurer in service of the id. The id initiates. From another point of view, social agreement is seen as springing from social intercourse, and social intercourse is based on language that has been, to some extent, developed rationally. But the behavior of the individual is molded by group will. From still another point of view, the habits built by the conditioning psychologist may be regarded as having developed because of the animal's ability to use its rational powers to learn; however, its behavior is shaped by the treatment it receives. In each of these theoretical orientations, rational influence is not omitted, but it is not viewed as a primary behavior determinant.

The lack of emphasis on man as a rational being and the tendency to focus on biological, social, and physical forces instead are responsible for certain limitations in the prevailing understanding of human behavior. An emphasis on desire as the primary determinant might suggest that hedonism is the pursuit of adjustment. A social approach might offer a basis for understanding the forces that influence us to behave like almost everybody else and provide criteria for identifying those of us who do not. But from this bias, deviation is often viewed as a problem and is seldom viewed as a measure of the volition exercised by a strong, self-willed individual. On the other hand, the physical emphasis focuses on the effect of physical stimuli on the postural motor responses of the organism, only touching lightly on rational process. There is, therefore, reason to believe that much can be learned concerning

The Theory: An Orientation

human behavior by focusing on the rational determinant rather than on the more conventional physical, biological, and social orientations.

While man obviously exists as a biological organism within a social group in a physical world, theorists in the past have hesitated to begin their work by positioning him as an intellectual, rational organism differing from other organisms chiefly in his rational capacity. The desirability of the rational has not been slighted; people respect rationality. From the beginning of history, philosophers have attempted to formulate the ideal rational society, but the explicit theoretical identification of rationality as a dynamic (or *the* dynamic) determinant of human behavior has been bypassed. The theory offered in the following chapters seeks to redress this comparative neglect. The orientation (and the bias) of the theory, therefore, is avowedly rational.

Although rationality will be discussed throughout the book, it may be helpful to provide the reader with an early reference to the term that will make clear the bias of the theory even though a theoretical context has not yet been provided and the term is not neatly qualified. *An individual is behaving rationally when he conceives predictions about observable events and tests them through observations.* The mind conceives predictions and assesses the validity of these predictions against ensuing events. Conceiving and testing predictions against events permits the individual to gain control or mastery of his relationship with the environment. The operation of the mind cannot be understood without reference to events.

Man, like any organism, is in a ceaseless quest for satisfaction. But more than any other creature, man is born helpless, with a poverty of both instincts and physical skills. At the same time, he has a unique potential for the use of his mind. Thus, man must develop his ability to predict and control himself in his environment as a means of acquiring satisfaction. Moreover, he is motivated to predict and control. He finds that learning to predict and control is satisfying because of its implications for predicting and controlling satisfaction in the future. The result is a predisposition to find prediction and control of any kind satisfying.

6

Man, therefore, is quite naturally inquisitive and experimental. Children play school, doctor, or house, while adults play more abstract games such as bridge or chess or solve crossword puzzles; both are, in a real sense, engaging in rehearsals for life.

The relationship between the individual's view of rationality and that of society should also be mentioned in this introduction to rationality. Man and the society in which he lives are in conflict about things. Perhaps the classic example is the conflict between the desires of the individual and the expectations of his society. There is, however, a crucial area of agreement between them: both hold that rationality is a highly desirable personal attribute. If a person is unable to predict and control himself in his environment, he can be of little value to himself or his society. Not only is the individual motivated to learn to predict and control, but society is likewise motivated to teach him to predict and control so that he may make social contributions.

Although defined in many ways, learning is always thought of as manifested by change over a period of time. The rational approach of the present theory can be delimited further in relation to the other three determinants by comparing their influence as the individual matures. For this purpose, let us consider the four behavior determinants on an axis moving from birth to maturity.

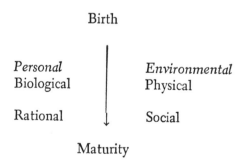

At birth the personal influences acting on the infant are predominantly biological drives relating to survival (e.g., hunger). The environmental influences are predominantly physical (e.g., food). As time passes, the infant learns to recognize the people who minister to his needs and soon comes under their influence. As this happens, the social influences in the environment become increasingly important. The infant learns to satisfy the expectations of society in order to ensure his survival. He placates the members of society (who control his survival) by using his rational powers to learn their language. He behaves differently when he becomes an adult, however. Some of the social values he once learned in order to ensure survival are now more precious than survival. He may be willing to die for his country. Biological impetuosity has been replaced by enough rationality and suppression of desire for him to hold a job, be a dutiful club member, be a model father—and problem-solve (e.g., play cards with his friends).

The above discussion may seem to labor heavily on society's influences, so that the reader may now wonder whether I am not, in fact, re-emphasizing the social in the form of rational development. Starting with the bias of the proposed theory in the direction of the rational component of the mind, am I not driven by my own logic to a second bias embracing the social determinant of behavior?

The answer is that while no major determinant can be ignored, the emphasis of the present work includes the social in only a rather special way. Society is not viewed as the dictator of the individual's life pattern but, rather, as the source of information and procedures that are important ingredients in the development of personal autonomy. The rational component of behavior depends for its growth not only on the individual's innate capacity for mastery but also on society's substantive contribution to the individual's rational machinery. A moment's reflection will help us distinguish this type of social influence from the social determinism of theories whose bias is primarily social.

In the present theory, in contrast to social determinism, the alleged conflict between the individual and society is, if not reconciled, at least seen in a new light in which the individual and society may share a most crucial concern for the same objective. That goal is the effective autonomy of strong individuals, able to steer themselves accurately in a direction compatible with—

indeed, essential to—the welfare of other people. The use of information and procedures inherited from one's society increases the individual's autonomy and the possibility of his making a social contribution. The individual who can predict and control can choose whether he wishes to conform or deviate and can appraise the consequences of either action. The advantage of this theory over social determinism is that it accounts more realistically for the phenomenon of individual choice and responsibility. Apart from the primary importance of these concepts in the value system of our culture, the occurrence of constructive "deviation" is more clearly explained by a focus on individual rationality than by the embarrassing gap such deviation leaves in the otherwise solid wall of social-deterministic theory.

The focus of some personality theories has been on man's quest for pleasure, which he supposedly gains only in his personal life. His work is viewed as a means to this end, and he is alleged to spend his working hours only in the hope of being done with them so that he can escape to fulfill his desires and passions. Perhaps the phrase *pursuit of happiness* has led us to the sterile notion that man works only to achieve leisure, a view that misses the whole point of man's most concentrated hours. What is more obvious about man than the formal, work-oriented, mental frameworks within which his most memorable achievements, and the very elaboration of society itself, have occurred? Why is it impossible to conceive of a love of work as a fact of life? One can only have a love of work if the work engages the mind in productive purposes. Work that is productive without engaging the mind is alienating, and work that engages the mind without being productive is pointless. Freud spoke of love and work as two of man's most important primary motives. One of these has been perverted and debased, the other almost totally neglected. The characteristic thing about gratifying work is the demands it places on rationality.

If we are to view our species realistically, the plain fact of rationally dominated behavior cannot be neglected or taken for granted, and the theorist's task is precisely to account for this predominant, mental behavior of the species. If the emphasis of

The Theory: An Orientation

theories of human behavior is on those characteristics that are shared by infrahumans (rage, hunger, sex, fright, for example), there is serious danger of confounding the investigation. I am not suggesting that existing theories of human behavior do, in fact, mistake rats for men but that generalizing from rats to humans is a very risky business. In fact, in existing theory, the tremendous possible leverage of human rationality has not been exploited. The present work is intended as a step in the direction of making explicit a dynamic factor that is, at best, vague, implicit, or peripheral in previous theoretical formulations.

Some theories stress what man shares with all animals; some, what he shares with some other animals. The theory proposed here is consistent with these accounts, but it stresses what appears to be especially human. A therapeutic focus on maladaptive behavior, for example, may easily mistake the part for the whole, at least in practice. One may say that a psychotic is irrational when, in fact, he may solve successfully a problem in integral calculus. It is precisely the overwhelming rationality of all human behavior that requires elucidation and that provides unused leverage for therapeutic and educational procedures.

The purpose of this book is not to explain why the rational has been neglected or to identify the neurological basis for rationality but, rather, to investigate the yield of a psychological approach that views rationality as an initiating force, a cause of behavior. This is what is meant by rationally determined behavior. However, it may be of value to review briefly some possible reasons for the neglect in order to outline the scope and nature of the problem to be dealt with throughout this book.

For one thing, man is still very sensitive about his rational prowess. The desirability of intelligence is so heavily weighted that he is fearful of being called stupid. This fear, coupled with the responsibility he must assume by admitting that he is the director of his own affairs, increases the threat associated with acknowledging rationality. Why risk rational responsibility when a moral or appetitive justification for an act can remove this threat? It may well be more difficult for man to accept his rationality than to face his greeds and lusts.

BACKGROUND

The admission that man's behavior is rationally determined carries with it a responsibility that man is reluctant to assume. To admit that his rational choices affect his behavior is to strip him of a protective covering of excuses. Man's tendency to surrender volition for dependency has been elaborated in various psychological treatises.

Some psychologists may consider the emphasis on rationality as naïve, in view of signs of irrationality at every turn, from academic debates to global cataclysms. Such psychologists, granting that there is indeed a rational component in the conduct of both scholarly affairs and world conflicts, may consider that a stress on rationality would nevertheless set psychology back at least three-quarters of a century by disregarding the vast insights into man's macabre depths that began with Freud's first publication. Moreover, before Freudian psychology was introduced into Western culture, it was necessary for man to attach moral justification to his deeds in order for them to be socially accepted. As time passed, hedonism became less objectionable. Now, when an individual says he acted as he did simply because he felt like it, he may be admired as self-directed and honest.

Another explanation to consider is that the rational component of human behavior is so obvious that it tends to be overlooked. The neurotic successfully finds his way to the psychiatrist's office in a metropolitan maze that would defy the most intelligent white rat, successfully communicates his troubles in an intricate symbolic code, and has no difficulty in interpreting the bill that reaches him at the end of the month. Man goes into space with a technical aplomb surpassing by a thousand times the aeronautical accomplishments of the most dexterous bird. These achievements —some celebrated, some taken totally for granted—are accomplished despite a poverty of instinctual and physical equipment that would leave any other animal totally helpless. Perhaps these achievements have become too commonplace to be noticed.

Still another—and perhaps the overriding—reason for the neglect of rationality in the study of behavior is the difficulty of studying rationality rationally. The theorist's equipment for the task is the very phenomenon to be investigated. There is no reason to suppose that man cannot be rational about rationality, but there are clearly special difficulties in the dual role of observed and observer from the point of view of bias and detachment.

Finally, mental process itself is obviously among the most complex functions known to man. Neither a priori reasoning about it nor empirical study of the brain has ever yielded cogent answers.

An espousal of the rational determinant does not mean that other determinants of human behavior are unimportant or irrelevant. The existing literature of behavioral theory offers impressive evidence to the contrary. Indeed, man's strength and his survival in the world of physically stronger, faster, and more numerous creatures can hardly be explained without detailed and realistic reference to his remarkable mind. In discussions of I.Q., for example, it is easy to assume that persons with a "low" I.Q. are unintelligent, when in fact an I.Q. of sixty places any human being far beyond the reaches of infrahuman intelligence. Such an individual, among chimpanzees, would be an Einstein.

To analyze man's rationality another way, studies of man can stress respects in which he is like all other animals (he can learn habits), he is like some other animals (he can walk and give you his paw), and he is like no other animals (he can talk). I am interested in the latter two distinctions. I am dealing with man as he is capable of creating realities never seen before (the electric light, spaceships). Man need not adapt to his environment or perish like other animals; he can mold his environment to suit himself. He need not grow a heavy coat of fur in the winter; he has only to adjust his thermostat to keep as warm as he wishes.

Previous theories, in contrast, often focus, quite legitimately, on man's similarity to other animals. The sociologists, Freudians, and learning theorists, for instance, all focus on habits. Sociologists study conformity—group habits. Freudians study the breaking of infantile habits that remain to haunt the adult. Learning theorists study how contiguity, punishment, and reward affect habits. But consider for a moment the maximum yield of habit as a framework for the analysis of behavior. Habit represents the influence of the past on the present; with habits, a man's future is, in a very real sense, his past. With the operation of rational intelligence, however, man is not so circumscribed. He can let the future mold the present. He can educate his children. He can draw plans for the future and begin to realize them in the present.

Deliberation—to which extended attention will be given in the following pages—occurs simply because an unfamiliar stimulus will not, in general, elicit a habit. Man's excellence consists precisely in his capacity to deal with the unfamiliar. Habits represent the heavy hand of the past shaping the present. Deliberation can prepare man to act in the present in order to achieve future aspirations never before realized. The height of this art is the invention of something previously unfamiliar to all men.

In all that follows, then, the stress will be on the predominance of rational behavior. However unreasonable man may appear at moments, there is always method in his madness, and it is the examination of this method that will concern us in this book. What are the mechanisms of rationality? How does it begin and, once begun, how does it work? Is there a basis for a rational psychology?

2

Views on Rationality

Although theorists in the biological, social, and physical traditions do not view rationality as an initiating force in human behavior, neither do they, in general, ignore it. The term *rationality* is rarely used by them, but a variety of partial synonyms is commonly encountered: thought, judgment, intelligence, conceptualization, cognition. Still other terms have a related meaning within the terminology of particular theorists—for example, Freud's *reality principle*. Thus, it seems both necessary and appropriate to present a general review of the more prominent views on rationality before proceeding to a theory that takes this particular aspect of human behavior as its central focus. The theory can then be developed without repeated references to other writers.

All psychologists acknowledge some kind of inaccessible activity within the organism. (The "black box" or empty-organism doctrines, which suggest that the central nervous system links stimulus and response but does not substantially influence the response, do not seem to be seriously held by anyone, though some workers feel that they can operate effectively without any more knowledge than these positions would imply.) If there were nothing in the organism, there would be nothing for psychology to investigate. Man would be comparable to a stone or a statue. No separate theory would be necessary, precisely because man would act in accordance with general laws of chemistry and inertia (as do stones and statues) and with no other laws. However, when an object has internal articulation of any kind, as certain machines do, more complicated formulations of physics must be invoked to account for the movements of the object (e.g., dynamics). In the case of a machine, these can be specified quite easily. The same is true, but with mounting complexity, for animate objects. Biology can give us an adequate account of the "behavior" of a fern, but we would not presume to deal scientifically with a fern by external observation alone. As an organism moves up the phylogenetic scale, the intricacy of its internal processes increases, and the effect of those processes on behavior likewise grows. Physical, chemical, and biological laws that apply to lower creatures still apply, but predictions become increasingly inaccurate as the presence of other laws produces interferences with those appropriate at lower levels. For the present viewpoint, the phylogenetic scale may be regarded as a hierarchy of unpredictability of behavior, the behavior of higher organisms being more unpredictable than that of lower organisms. Higher animals are not exempt from general laws of behavior that apply to inorganic matter and lower forms of life. Laws of behavior peculiar to the higher animals, therefore, must be very potent indeed to increase as they do the inaccuracy of predictions based on more general laws. This unpredictability, I believe, is attributable to internal interference.

Our most certain knowledge that man differs from the rat is derived from the fact that laws of rodent behavior, carefully accumulated in the laboratory, are of low predictive value for human behavior, signifying substantial interference. In speaking of rationality, I have in mind a source of this internal interference. From a scientific point of view, therefore, man's rationality is a source of "lawlessness"; in the present state of knowledge, it reduces our capacity to predict natural phenomena. (The fact that rationality is also the factor within us that enables us to do our predicting is beside the point.)

If human behavior could be neatly associated and correlated with stimulation, psychologists could close shop and leave the matter in the hands of other scientists. What tends to confuse the issue is that man's behavior *can* be predicted under highly artificial conditions. We can predict that a man will die under certain conditions, that he will sleep if given certain drugs, and that he will bleed if pricked. This entices us to believe that by refining our control of stimulation sufficiently, we can predict all human behavior.

The type of behavior that can be so predicted is what I shall call automatic behavior. Not only can the kneejerk be predicted, but many actions that clearly seem to involve mental functions can also be predicted with exactly the accuracy with which habits can be identified and relied on. Statistically, this covers large segments of human performance. It falls short of total predictive success to the extent that it becomes deliberate behavior, which I shall identify in later chapters.

Automatic behavior is stimulus-dominated, often externally initiated. So long as stimuli are carefully selected and the state of the organism is carefully controlled, this behavior may reach almost any desired level of predictability. But the selection of such stimuli must systematically exclude many stimuli that appear to be characteristic of the habitat of species at the upper end of the phylogenetic scale. As laboratory conditions approach in realism the habitat of the species, prediction only by external observation decreases in precision, an occurrence that does not exist in the case of the stone and is not important in our understanding of the fern (once we know its internal structure). If the aberrant behavior produced by more "natural" stimulation were slight, the issue would not, in the balance, be serious. As it happens, however, the deviations involved in deliberate behavior are precisely in the behavioral areas that concern us most. Most of the behavior we can predict best by external observation tends to be of a mechanical sort that least satisfies our curiosity, while the rich and exotic complex behavior that interests us most remains stubbornly resistant to prediction. Such would be the case with the fern if we had no notion of the cell or how sunlight and water are used to produce chlorophyll—whence biology comes to our rescue with a conceptual scheme that accounts for the fern's "behavior."

As an explanation for human behavior, the notion of the cell alone seems quite inadequate, although it is just as necessary as stone-level chemistry is to the cellular account of the fern. That is to say, we must have, in acounting for human behavior, at least chemistry and the cell. The leap from these solid concepts to such an apparently esoteric idea as rationality is occasioned only by the obvious need for some such unifying concepts as Hebb sought in the "cell assembly" and the "phase sequence" to introduce some explanatory order into the extreme diversity of human conduct.[1] The gap acknowledged by Hebb between "neurologizing" and "psychologizing" is one that every serious contemporary psychologist has tried to narrow by constructs analogous to what is more definitely known. Rationality makes its claim among constructs as a principle of high generality in accounting for deliberate behavior while remaining consistent with the acknowledged data of reflexive behavior.

In reviewing the literature on the influence of the rational on man's behavior, two problems are evident immediately. First, there is the matter of theoretical bias as discussed in chapter 1; few, if any, theorists have focused on rationality as a primary behavior determinant. Second, many psychologists have limited their studies to simpler forms of behavior, or to the behavior of organisms less complicated than man (and even then under very limited or artificial conditions), thus reducing the burden of explanation. The rational is then slighted through methodology. The explanation of behavior is a difficult matter, and the psychologist tends to retreat to the safety of the laboratory. Thus, methodological limitations represent a large factor in the summary that follows.

Allport finds fault with the appeal to methodological limitations. He states: "Precisely here we find the reason why so many psychologists fail to take an interest in the existential richness of human life. Methods, they say, are lacking. . . . [They have preference for] a passive, reactive organism rather than for one that is spontaneous and active."[2] But Spence, taking what is perhaps an extreme position, defends the practice of dealing with behavior that can be treated in a publicly verifiable, reproducible way, in these terms: "the criterion that has guided us in any

[1] Donald O. Hebb, *The Organization of Behavior.*
[2] Gordon W. Allport, *Becoming,* pp. 11–12.

priorities . . . has been our estimate of the likelihood of successful accomplishment of our aim of discovering scientific laws about the phenomena. Being guided by such purely scientific objectives and not having any special interests, humanitarian, religious, social betterment or otherwise, no particular area of human or animal behavior is seen as more important than another."[3] It could be argued, of course, that according to Spence's reasoning one could enumerate thousands of trivial "laws" of behavior more easily verified than those in the Spence formulations. For example, one could enumerate—species by species, and subspecies by subspecies—the tendencies to retreat from fire. There is much to be said, however, for the type of objectivity Spence represents as against centuries of noncumulative verbalizations about behavior. The productivity of science has certainly resulted from the conviction that it is better to know a few things than to guess at many and know none. This is particularly so if there is no conceivable way of advancing from one's guesses to any knowledge of their validity.

Indeed, the two factors of theoretical bias and methodology seem to be the main determinants of the positions that will be discussed. All roads in behavioral theory must pass through rationality. The various theorists, however, depending on prior interest or attachment to some productive method, will either choose a route through the suburbs or, if necessary, get through the heart of town as rapidly as possible. Very few care to stay over and do any sightseeing.

Large-scale efforts to deal with rationality directly have been contained in treatments by Johnson, Bartlett, and Bruner, Goodnow, and Austin. Johnson's treatment, unjustifiably ignored in most of the literature (except by Mowrer), makes no attempt to be theoretical but, rather, chooses usefully to "organize what is known about each section of the field and to push a short distance into the unknown."[4] Johnson points out that, based on his review of 740 pertinent references, up to 1955, "To anyone with a practical or theoretical interest in human beings the status of the

---

[3] Kenneth W. Spence, *Behavior Theory and Learning*, pp. 79–80.
[4] Donald M. Johnson, *The Psychology of Thought and Judgment*, p. ix.

psychology of thought is distressing. Such fields of psychology as perception, learning, and personality are being explored thoroughly and systematically. The science of psychology may be proud of current progress in these fields. But the scientific investigation of thinking is unsystematic and, in general, unsatisfactory."[5] Johnson's own taxonomic approach does not shed much light on either the origins or, in his phrase, the "improvement of thinking." Under the latter rubric he offers such common-sense recommendations as that the thinker can "open a window" and "soundproof the walls" or "adopt a set to attend to some things and ignore others."

Bartlett's treatment is theoretically somewhat more substantive, but he was not interested in producing "anything like a systematic treatise."[6] He treats thought under two general categories, "thinking within closed systems" and "adventurous thinking." The latter he divides into "the thinking of the experimental scientist," "everyday thinking," and "the artist's thinking."[7] He defines thinking in general as "the extension of evidence in accord with that evidence so as to fill gaps in the evidence. . . . this is done by moving through a succession of interconnected steps which may be stated at the time, or left till later to be stated."[8] This definition, it will be seen, bears some relation to Bruner's notion of conceptualization and to such Gestalt notions as closure and the "good Gestalt." Significantly, Bartlett stresses also the "direction" of thought, a notion with which the present volume tries to deal more explicitly.[9]

Of closed-system thinking, Bartlett says, "one of the most characteristic features . . . is that, as the number of steps taken towards filling up a gap increases, the number of probable next steps decreases, until a stage in the sequence is reached beyond which all thinking must proceed through the same number and order of steps to the same terminus." He finds this also characteristic of

[5] Ibid., p. 1.
[6] Frederick Bartlett, *Thinking*, p. 8.
[7] Ibid., p. 9.
[8] Ibid., p. 75.
[9] Ibid., p. 76.

"experimental scientific investigation," in the "sense that once a halting-place has been scientifically justified, as it is neared the steps to it become more and more the same for everybody." Everyday thinking, on the other hand, operates in such a way that "the end of the preferred argument sequence itself takes charge of the selection of particular items of evidence, which are then used as if they set up the sequence leading to the issue accepted." Artistic thinking is such that "the step sequence [effected] . . . is never one which converges steadily to a single issue. In its earlier stages every step opens up more diverging paths. Later, characteristically, it reaches some critical stage beyond which each successive step achieves a partial issue which presents itself as the one that is most satisfying, but never as the only possible one. [Its] . . . terminus will appear inevitable to all those who accept and understand the artist's standard; but it will not without search display an answer to all the questions that can still be legitimately raised."[10]

Bartlett's views, while interesting, seem to be easily vulnerable to a variety of difficult questions. There seems, first, to be nothing immutable about the convergence of scientific thinking, since results, even within mathematics, are periodically upset by later thinking; what, then, sets their inevitability? Second, the notions of "standard" and "satisfying" seem both vague and inadequate to account for the compelling quality of inventive thinking. Third, it is not clear whether Bartlett includes invention under "artistic" thinking or indeed includes it at all. It is true that theorizing tends to be "satisfying," but this is hardly enough to keep it alive. At the same time, theories are notoriously perishable but nonetheless useful on that account. Whence comes their utility? How does one explain, in Bartlett's terms, heuristics or even simple analogy?

Bruner, Goodnow, and Austin offer an analysis of "conceptualization" as a process of categorizing. ". . . categorizing serves to cut down the diversity of objects and events that must be dealt with uniquely by an organism of limited capacities and . . . makes possible the sorting of functionally significant groupings in

[10] Ibid., pp. 190–91, 191, 175, 198.

the world. . . . One goes beyond this . . . to . . . categorizing strategies."[11] The stress in this account is on information processing—that is, how to make the world simple enough to be dealt with. ". . . virtually all cognitive activity involves and is dependent on the process of categorizing. More critical still, the act of categorizing derives from man's capacity to infer from sign to signicate. . . ."[12] In a discussion that parallels some of the discussions of "properties" in symbolic logic (e.g., Rudolf Carnap, *Meaning and Necessity*), Bruner, Goodnow, and Austin offer an impressive analysis of the process of selecting useful common traits from raw experience in order to make such experience manageable. In behavioristic terms (a point of view not invoked by these authors), this work could be considered a monumental study of "stimulus generalization," and as such it is invaluable in its utility and the merit of its detail, but a serious question exists as to whether this restricted topic justifies the title of their book. Categorizing is only one aspect of thought.

Up to now there seem to be no other large-scale contemporary analyses of rationality within a psychological framework. Classical treatments, such as Dewey's in *How We Think*, are subjective or purely formal. It should be noted, however, that Dewey's description of "reflective experience" bears some resemblance to the treatment of problem solving being presented here.

Among the treatments outside the framework of psychology, formal logic, of course, looms largest. Newell, Shaw, and Simon have suggested that the connection between symbolic logic and the human process of proof is, in fact, very close. The subject, in their experimentation, was not a human being but a computer, which was given the task of "proving" the first fifty-two theorems in Russell and Whitehead's *Principia Mathematica*. They programmed into the computer the axioms of the PM system (as it is commonly known) and four logical rules of inference: substitution, replacement, detachment, and syllogism (or chaining). As

[11] Jerome S. Bruner, Jacqueline J. Goodnow, and George A. Austin, A *Study of Thinking*, p. 246.
[12] Ibid.

an example of the four rules (all tautological), let us take the last, chaining. According to this rule, if *a* implies *b*, and if *b* implies *c*, then *a* implies *c*. The result of the experiment was that the computer "proved" about 75 percent of the theorems, taking from as little time as eight seconds to as much as forty-five minutes per theorem. In the process, according to the authors, they produced analogs of the psychological processes of "set" and "insight."[13]

As a result of setting a noncomputational task, the authors seem to have refuted by their experiment those who regard computers as idiotic computational geniuses. Computers can also be programmed to compose poems and play checkers. Thus, the mind and the computer can perform some of the same tasks. However, without man to initiate and direct the activities of the computer, it does nothing. The fact seems to be that man has invented the computer to relieve himself of the burden of performing tasks that the computer can perform more rapidly and accurately.

I now proceed in this review to the traditional battleground of twentieth-century psychology—the opposition between behaviorism and cognitivism. These two contrasting main currents of modern psychology have approached the problem in different ways.

The first, launched by John B. Watson early in the century, retains its vitality to the present under the name of behaviorism, which denotes a technique as well as a class of theory. The second, emanating from Germany, is the Gestalt movement, which, through numerous transformations, now appears as one of the foundations of the cognitivist position. Related to the second movement, in granting status to internal processes, is phenomenology, which takes natural behavior (as opposed to controlled behavior) as it is, in its gross visible forms, and does not hesitate to deal with it at this observable, common-sense, molar level. The first of these views is largely "physical"; the second, largely "biological"

[13] Allen Newell, John C. Shaw, and Herbert A. Simon, "Elements of a Theory of Human Problem Solving."

and "social." The main problem of both is how to cope with rationality as a source of deliberate phenomena that often challenge current theorists' attempts at generality.

One solution is, in fact, to beg the question, refusing to deal with anything between stimulus input and response output. The simpler versions of this position seem hardly to be held today. Watson, Pavlov, and Thorndike are among the great early names in this kind of rejection of the question. Of the modern versions of behaviorism, the most celebrated is that of Skinner, whose closest approach to the question of rationality appears to be his treatment of thought in *Verbal Behavior*. Skinner tells us that the man who, when asked what he is doing, says " 'I'm just thinking' . . . is behaving . . . even though his behavior may not be easily observed by others or possibly even by himself. . . . It is tempting to avoid problems . . . by confining ourselves to observable events. . . . But there would then be certain embarrassing gaps in our account. When someone solves a problem in 'mental arithmetic,' the initial statement of the problem and the final overt answer can often be related only by inferring covert events." Skinner seems to find the nature of this relationship to be one of the "probability" of behavior without any "need to make guesses about the muscular or neural substratum. . . ." The notion of probability thus gives us a kind of public access to, and a means of dealing scientifically with, "operant" behavior, which "almost always begins in a form which affects the external environment, for it would not otherwise be reinforced." He explains the use of the term *almost* as allowing for certain responses that are automatically reinforced by the organism itself.[14]

"Operant behavior" (i.e., behavior without an obvious immediate stimulus) is Skinner's explanation of the various phenomena of rationality, and he contends that it can be dealt with only by an external determination of its likelihood. Essentially, then, while Skinner acknowledges that something happens between stimulus and response ("physiological processes mediate the probability of covert and overt responses alike . . . but we can

[14] B. F. Skinner, *Verbal Behavior*, pp. 434, 435.

talk about both forms of response . . . without identifying physiological mediators"), he chooses not to pursue the matter, for methodological reasons. "Thinking" is "behaving which automatically affects the behavior and is reinforcing because it does so." The thinker becomes an "adequate community" for "his own sustained production" (as in creative endeavors). Thinking "is not some mysterious process responsible for behavior but the very behavior itself in all the complexity of its controlling relations." These views are more sophisticated than earlier expositions of behaviorism, but they still clearly reject "unknown" internal processes both as a legitimate subject of scientific inquiry at this time and as, in any sense, a "determinant" of behavior. "So far as a science of behavior is concerned, Man Thinking is simply Man Behaving."[15]

Skinner's views are inadequate, however, to account for the complexity of verbal behavior or to predict it with any cogency. Skinner does not solve the problem he poses but merely adds some new terminology, such as his concept of the "mand," or self-stimulating verbal act, which says nothing about what form the verbal act will take (that is, what words will be used, in what order, with what inflections, and on what occasions). Skinner says that "in representing the relationships discovered by an experimental analysis of behavior, little use is made of metaphors or analogies drawn from other sciences. Reports seldom contain expressions like *encode, read out from storage, reverberating circuits* . . . or *cell assemblies.*"[16] It is not at all clear, however, that nonoperational neologisms like "mand" or mere statements of identity between thinking and behaving serve a purpose any more effective in escaping current methodological limitations. At the present stage of knowledge, it would be desirable to evade statistically the difficult gap provided by internal processes. Neither Skinner nor anyone else, however, has carried out this work in attempting to account successively for the deliberate behavior of individuals.

[15] Ibid., pp. 435, 438, 439, 449, 452.
[16] B. F. Skinner, "What Is the Experimental Analysis of Behavior?," p. 217.

Estes provides an extended summary of efforts in this direction, but admits that "formulation of a stimulus trace model within statistical learning theory [is still] . . . in the future."[17] In his extended treatment (over 100 pages) in *Psychology: A Study of a Science*, for which comments on "intervening variables" were invited by the editor, Estes did not avail himself of the opportunity.

More intricate attempts, within a framework that can be roughly classified as behavioristic, have been made by several major psychologists to account for the gap by means of intervening variables, a concept credited to E. C. Tolman. The most sophisticated and celebrated of these views is Clark L. Hull's system, as set forth in *A Behavior System*. Here an attempt is made to quantify the influence of intervening variables on observed behavior. Unfortunately, this quantification is entirely arbitrary, with values chosen on the basis of mathematical convenience. The effect is a set of propositions of impressively precise nature, whose precision, however, is of nonempirical origin. Such formulations involve a special and serious danger. Unless one notes Hull's conscientious acknowledgment of the nonempirical selection of numerical values, one is apt to believe that the precision represents actual empirical affairs within the organism. Hull further classifies his propositions according to whether they have or have not been empirically verified. The most that appears to have been verified, however, is a greater tendency to behave (postural behavior) in one way than in another—and, again, always in the context of relatively simple stimulation. It does not appear, therefore, that Hull has advanced beyond Skinner's attempt at statistical evasion of the "thinking gap," and the statistical results are in any case inadequate to provide explanations or predictions of the kinds of behavior that interest us most—what lies between stimulus and response. Hull speaks deferentially of the "great problem" of thinking, but nothing in

[17] William K. Estes, "The Statistical Approach to Learning Theory," pp. 461–62.

his system, or in Spence's elaborations of the system, offers much promise of dealing successfully with this "great problem."[18]

Spence characteristically eschews any meaning in an intervening variable, dividing himself from Hull's use of "physiological connotations" and insisting only on their "mathematical specifications." "The type of theoretical schema that employs intervening variables, as I conceive it," he states, "is primarily concerned with integrating and bringing into deductive relation with one another the different, specific laws found in the various kinds of learning situations."[19] Indeed, as a general commentary on the entire "modified behaviorist" approach to the explanation of higher human mental functions, probably nothing can serve better than the following observation by the inventor of the intervening variables: "I am now convinced that 'intervening variables' to which we attempt to give merely operational meaning by tying them through empirically grounded functions either to stimulus variables, on the one hand, or to the response variables, on the other, can give us no help unless we can also imbed them in a model from whose attributed properties we can deduct new relationships to be looked for."[20]

It is not my intention to impugn the usefulness of the concept of the intervening variable. Like the word *virus* in medicine, as it was originally used, it stands for that which we cannot explain in behavioral terms, and it is a reminder of the need for such explanation. The analogy is by no means complete, and the difference favors the concept of the virus, for we now know much about the environment of the virus, whereas the typical intervening variable is not based on empirically known aspects of central process. Several decades of attempts to come to any conclusions about these variables have proved unrewarding, and no one in the tradition has offered any reason to believe that

[18] Edward C. Tolman, *Purposive Behavior in Animals and Men*; Clark L. Hull, *A Behavior System*; Spence, *Behavior Theory and Learning*.

[19] Spence, p. 86.

[20] Tolman, quoted in Jerome S. Bruner and David Drech, eds., *Perception and Personality*, p. 49.

we are on the verge of a breakthrough. When thought is introduced into behavioristic accounts, it appears with all the lushness
and vagueness that have always characterized introspective treatments. Mowrer tells us that "at least in some types of thinking,
there is a process of self-stimulation and response involving the
subject-predicate relationship."[21] And Osgood is cited by Mowrer
as regarding "thought [as] involving 'light' [i.e., easy and *safe*]
responses which help the individual determine what course of
overt ['heavy,' important, fateful] action to pursue."[22] In short,
if we are to seek an explanation of mediating processes, we can
expect no more illumination from the behaviorists than to be
told that such processes exist and that no one seriously denies
them any more.

Let us now see if the second mainstream of psychological
thought in the twentieth century offers a more satisfactory version
of rationality. For purposes of discussion, this movement can be
divided loosely into Gestalt (field) and phenomenological trends.
The advocates of both trends acknowledge and focus on the
organism's internal processes by means of various external constructs, including social constructs.

The Gestaltists, also known at various times as cognitivists
and field theorists, began their work with a consideration of the
problems of perception; the major names in this tradition are
Wertheimer, Koffka, and Köhler. Lewin and Tolman are the
major figures in later, field-theory elaborations of the Gestaltist
view. The earlier theorists confined their discussions to perceptual
problems (that is, problems of recognition), and these discussions
are therefore not relevant to the question of rationality except
insofar as perception forms a foundation for any higher mental
operations. Hebb deals succinctly with the relation of this foundation to the views presented here. What Hebb says, in essence,
is that the Gestaltist view accounts for only certain phenomena of
perception, and that the Gestaltist view can be subsumed more
satisfactorily under the more inclusive concept of his cell-assembly

---

[21] Orval H. Mowrer, *Learning Theory and the Symbolic Process*, p. 224.
[22] Ibid., p. 214n.

view, which accounts for perception of all objects.[23]

Let us consider briefly the heart of the Gestalt view—the notion of the Gestalt itself. Closure, good continuation, and the other major subvarieties of the "good Gestalt" seem to suggest a structuring of some kind in the mind which, like the Kantian category, fits data to its Procrustean bed. That is, organisms tend to recognize things as a function of their organization and presentation. Is this not to some extent a helpful approach to the understanding of the operation of the mind? The concept of Gestalt has clearly been useful in relation to perception.

The same does not seem to apply to thinking, however. Like Bruner's static taxonomy of concepts—useful in that it enumerates some of the simplifications achieved by the mind—the Gestalt is useful in illustrating what kinds of simplification of reality the mind achieves for its own purposes. But neither view tells us, in more than the most general way, why the mind accomplishes this simplification or—what is a more serious concern —how the mind does so. In short, it appears that pure Gestaltism has made only one major contribution to the psychology of thinking. It has called attention to some important data that call for explanation. It has not provided an explanation.

The same, in essence, could be said of Tolman and of Lewin, the Gestalt field theorists. Lewin gives us, as it were, a quantified road map, with the implication that the individual will go in one direction or another according to the quantifications on the map. Lewin himself uses the phrase *cognitive structure* but suggests, only in the most metaphorical manner, how this cognitive structure actually internalizes the surrounding polarities. Each of its "constructs," he suggests, "might be regarded as having the same dimension as position because it refers to the relative position of different parts of a field. Structure does not refer, however, to the position of one point but to the position of a multitude of points or regions."[24] The issue on which Lewin and the behaviorists seem to differ concerns the complexity of the stimulus.

[23] Hebb, pp. 17–59.
[24] Kurt Lewin, *Field Theory in Social Sciences*, pp. 33–40.

Where the behaviorist links a neutral (and most often a single) stimulus to a simple response, Lewin calls attention to the great complexity of stimuli impinging simultaneously on the organism. A response, then, is not a mere habit-link with the stimulus but, rather, a resultant of forces, by analogy with physics.

Now, if the polarities that Lewin assigns to the behavioral field were as explicit as the data of physics, we would indeed have a perfect device for predicting behavior with the same precision and subtlety that the engineer can apply in mechanics. Unfortunately, like Hull's quantification, Lewin's analysis is an overstatement. It lacks an empirical base. The important forces in an individual's psychological field are simply not determinable without a state of knowledge about the human mind which, if we had it, would render Lewin's theory less necessary and should certainly be more accurate for predictive purposes. If field theory could actually bypass questions of internal process, the utility of Lewinian polarity concepts would be of inestimable value, but Lewin offers us no promising means of assigning such polarities. A further difficulty in this view is the excessive problem of deciding what things, exactly, are to be quantified. Therefore, Lewinian methodologists are obliged to apply unknown quantities to unknown things. This can hardly help in the prediction or control of behavior.

Field-theory doctrine does, however, seem to offer some hints, at least, with respect to the explanation of behavior. We perceive, from our intuitive knowledge of ourselves, that we are variously impelled in various directions; the impelling forces are, as we will see, of various magnitudes. What determines action, however, is valence, not vector. Lewin recognizes qualities within the organism, such as needs, but he then displays them in his "life space" as the attractiveness of objects—that is, as valences. In the balance, however, Lewin's views seem to represent a provocative metaphor, misleadingly quantitative, rather than a workable model of psychological processes.

A final word on Gestalt theory should be devoted to the important term *insight*, which, though it antedates (in English) the Gestaltists by some four centuries, would probably not have its present currency except for its crucial role in Gestaltist writings;

and I believe it was intended to deal with more than recognition. The positing of insight and what it implies is the Gestaltists' contribution to the understanding of the complexities of thought that are related to prompt learning. Within the Gestaltist frame of reference, insight appears to call attention to something in need of further explanation, rather than to explain it fully. Still, particular credit is due the Gestaltists for this concept of insight, which goes well beyond the problems of perception.

This leads the discussion to the phenomenologists—in which camp I am grouping (without their consent) a diverse and miscellaneous collection of major theorists who have in common only a lack of interest in the epistemological conundrums of the behaviorists and cognitivists. Like the cognitivists, they have no quarrel with "internal" states of mind. (In fact, this lack of concern with how we actually know what is going on in the mind could be alleged as a weakness common to all the various views I shall cite.) The theorists in question—psychiatrists and sociologists, as well as a number of professional psychologists— have all started with what, from their point of view, are more pressing problems or theoretically more interesting ones. Sociologists, for instance, can hardly afford to wait until psychology settles its internal differences or they would obviously have to choose different careers; neither can psychiatrists postpone all appointments until psychological theory is complete—although they would then have more justification for keeping them. The psychotherapists and the sociologists suffer from the same psychological vacuum I have been discussing—namely, how central process operates empirically in all of its complexity. Psychotherapists must validate their influence on their subjects by noting internal changes. Sociologists can measure the effects of social constraints only if they can assess consistent behavior among persons subject to the same social pressures that act as a constant.

In completing this review of previous studies of rationality, I shall look briefly at the work of those who deal primarily with the individual as well as of those who look at the individual from the perspective of society.

Muenzinger, credited by Mowrer with having originated the notion of "VTE" (vicarious trial and error) as a model for thinking, has offered in this concept a notion of rational process that bears some relation to this discussion. In one experiment Muenzinger demonstrated effectively the tendency of thought to seek to eliminate itself and issue into action. It appears, according to Muenzinger's theories, that thought *precedes* habit in a manner which I shall characterize as the tendency of deliberation to relegate to reflexive behavior those matters no longer needing its attentions.[25]

Osgood, Suci, and Tannenbaum have conducted celebrated investigations into the nature of meaning, via what they term the *semantic differential* by which a semantic space is defined. They find three factors determining this semantic space: evaluation, potency, and activity. Examples of the first factor would be good versus bad, clean versus dirty; of the second, strong versus weak, large versus small; of the third, active versus passive, fast versus slow, and so forth. The experimental subjects, in the methodology of Osgood and his collaborators, are presented with lists of words to which they are asked to react in terms of the "semantic scale" of polar pairs of values. The result seems to be that certain public concepts have typical "semantic space" for the typical subject, indicating, according to Osgood, that something basic in human thinking is being uncovered.[26]

Despite the celebrated nature of these studies, I cannot share Osgood's optimism that something basic in human thinking is being revealed. It is a *result* of thinking that is being revealed. What really seems to be at issue here is what is commonly called the connotation of a word; thus, the word *father* may less frequently evoke the response "good" than the word *mother* does, even though the alleged basic meanings of the two words have no ethical implications. A common linguistic criticism of this work by Osgood and his coauthors is that it does not deal with the basic meaning—or referent—of the terms presented to its subjects,

[25] Karl F. Muenzinger and Evelyn Gentry, "Tone Discrimination in White Rats"; Orval H. Mowrer, *Learning Theory and the Symbolic Process*, p. 212; Muenzinger, *Reward and Punishment*.

[26] Charles E. Osgood, George J. Suci, and Percy H. Tannenbaum, *The Measurement of Meaning*.

and that it consequently does not come to grips with the primary problem in the notoriously troubled area of meaning. In view of the title of the study, this criticism appears linguistically justified, and in any case it is difficult to see exactly what is meant by "semantic space" and exactly what implications it has for "something basic in human thinking." The authors tell us that "One can envisage the gradual construction of a functional dictionary of connotative meanings—a quantized thesaurus—in which the writer would find nouns, adjectives, adverbs (all lexical items) listed according to their locations in the semantic space, as determined from the judgments of representative samples of the population."[27] The utility of a volume such as this appears doubtful, especially since the parameters thus far used only scratch the surface of possibilities. Osgood's work does serve to illustrate the complex interrelations between language (our primary symbolic system) and human thought. The illustration, however, is not a solution to the problems it raises. Its ultimate significance may be in the area of diagnosis rather than in any explanation of language or of human behavior.

Let us now turn to a major investigator of human intellectual development, Jean Piaget. Piaget, making very limited theoretical claims (and ignoring questions of sampling and of statistical significance), has informally identified five stages of human development, as follows:

    I. Period of sensory-motor intelligence (0–2 years)

    II. Period of preconceptual thought (2–4 years): "preconcepts" (not decentered)

    III. Period of intuitive thought (4–7 years): e.g., evaluation of size of objects by greatest dimension

    IV. Period of concrete operations (7–11 years): operational thought

    V. Period of formal operations (11–15 years): child can deal hypothetically[28]

These stages are described operationally in Piaget's writings, but other researchers have not found the stages to occur with any

[27] Ibid., p. 330.
[28] D. E. Berlyne, "Recent Developments in Piaget's Work," pp. 1–12.

predictability at the ages specified by Piaget. Despite the lavish detail Piaget provides in his work, he offers little in the way of theoretical formulation of the nature of intelligence, assuming it, rather, as the basis for his specific work with children. For instance, in *The Origins of Intelligence in Children*, probably the only statements which could be construed as theoretical are the following: "The invention of new means through mental combination manifests all the characteristics of those rapid or even instantaneous regroupings . . . [of] the true act of intelligence."[29] And: "The simplest habits, as well as the so-called acquired 'associations' do not result from true associations, that is to say, interuniting the terms given as such, but also result from connections implying a structured totality from the outset."[30]

Piaget's work is of great interest for the practical understanding of intelligence in children. Some of his results are invoked here in a later chapter, in connection with the empirical implications of the present work. However, apart from his interesting *Logic and Psychology*, which contains a concise account of the progressive use of logical tools in thinking at the various stages outlined above, thus giving some substance to his contention that one stage presupposes the earlier ones, Piaget does not seem to have much to offer to a theory of rationality as a human behavioral determinant. His theoretical constructs, such as "accommodation, assimilation, and schema," refer to the way in which the individual passively adjusts to stimulation. These constructs are rather loosely extrapolated from his empirical observations. The following quotations from *The Growth of Logical Thinking from Childhood to Adolescence* give some notion of the relatively haphazard and capricious nature of Piaget's more abstract formulations:

. . . far from being a source of fully elaborated "innate" ideas, the maturation of the nervous system can do no more than determine the totality of possibilities and impossibilities at a given stage.

[29] Jean Piaget, *The Origins of Intelligence in Children*, p. 378.
[30] Ibid., p. 378.

. . . the psychological facts allow us to reject [the] hypothesis of social determinism.

We take as the fundamental problem of adolescence the fact that the individual begins to take up adult roles.

The child does not build systems. His spontaneous thinking may be more or less systematic . . . ; but it is the observer who sees the system from outside, while the child is not aware of it since he never thinks about his own thought.[31]

Piaget's merit is that he is specific—he has seen what he is talking about—and that he endeavors to be highly objective. In addition, he has carried the art of external manipulation to a high level of competence, although his procedures, as others have commented, make no effort to impose scientific controls. He is a careful taxonomist, using very few conceptual constructs to describe, but he offers little explanation as to why his subjects behave as they do. His progressive descriptions may be true on a grosser scale of levels than he proposes.

Indeed, the problem in reviewing Piaget in the present perspective is pervasive throughout the various writers we are now considering. Phenomenologists in general, while accepting rationality, deal with it in passing. Their emphasis is elsewhere, and the evidence of this portion of my review is, in fact, that most of these writers acknowledge it in one way or another, taking it for granted rather than attempting to cope with the problems it presents for acceptable model building in the understanding of human nature. White, for instance, maintains that the growth of children depends on "competence motivation," or effective interaction with the environment. Such "basic" motives as hunger and thirst satisfaction have more of a peripheral nature, the competence drive being the central motive.[32]

Reflecting a seeming tendency of psychologists of finally tiring of attempting to extrapolate from the rat to the human and increasingly committing themselves, at whatever methodological

[31] Baerbal Inhelder and Jean Piaget, *The Growth of Logical Thinking,* pp. 337, 338, 335, 339.
[32] Robert W. White, "Motivation Reconsidered."

risk, to the necessity of dealing somehow with man's more significant mental functions, some creativity studies have taken the unabashed position that "creativity" refers to a fairly specific type of cognitive ability. Like the intelligence tests of the past, whose basic assumptions are still unresolved, creativity-measuring devices are now flourishing, but none of them appears to have improved on Getzels and Jackson's demonstration that students high in creativity (whatever creativity may be) perform as well on achievement tests as those with high intelligence (whatever intelligence may be). The Getzels-Jackson research design, however, was good throughout; it was a safe pioneering approach to a long-neglected problem.[33]

In the same general tradition of subjectivity as White's "competence motivation," we have the very influential and articulate Abraham Maslow, who presented these views:

We have seen that instincts and flexible, cognitive adaptation to the novel tend to be mutually exclusive in the phyletic scale. The more of one we find, the less of the other we may expect. Because of this the vital and even tragic mistake (in view of the historical consequences) has been made from time immemorial, of dichotomizing instinctive impulse and rationality in the human being. It has rarely occurred to anyone that they might *both* be instinctoid in the human being, and more important, that their results or implied goals might be identical and synergic rather than antagonistic. . . . It is our contention that the impulses to know and to understand may be exactly as conative as the needs to belong or to love. . . . In the ordinary instinct-reason dichotomy or contrast, it is a badly defined instinct and a badly defined reason that are opposed to each other. If they were correctly defined in accordance with modern knowledge, they would be seen as not contrasting or opposing or even as strongly different from each other. . . . we assert instinctoid needs and rationality to be probably synergic and not antagonistic. Their apparent antagonism is an artifact produced by an exclusive preoccupation with sick people.[34]

---

[33] Jacob W. Getzels and Philip W. Jackson, *Creativity and Intelligence.*
[34] Abraham H. Maslow, *Motivation and Personality*, pp. 131–32.

Views on Rationality

Let us also consider briefly what the most celebrated of psychiatrists has to say about reason and rationality. Freud tells us that

the ego has the task of bringing the influence of the external world to bear upon the id and its tendencies, and endeavors to substitute the reality-principle for the pleasure-principle which reigns supreme in the id. In the ego, perception plays the part which in the id devolves upon instinct. *The ego represents what we call reason and sanity* [italics added]. All this . . . is only to be regarded as holding good in an average or "ideal" case.

The functional importance of the ego is manifested in the fact that normally control over the approaches to mobility devolves upon it. Thus in its relation to the id it is like a man on horseback, who has to hold in check the superior strength of the horse; with this difference, that the rider seeks to do so with his own strength while the ego uses borrowed forces. The illustration may be carried further. Often a rider, if he is not to be parted from his horse, is obliged to guide it where it wants to go; so in the same way the ego constantly carries into action the wishes of the id as if they were its own.[35]

He becomes even more explicit in the following statement:

We now see the ego in its strength and in its weaknesses. It is entrusted with important functions. By virtue of its relation to the perceptual system, it arranges the processes of the mind in a temporal order and tests their correspondence with reality. By interposing the process of thinking it secures a postponement of motor discharges and controls the avenues to motility. This last office is, to be sure, a question more of form than of fact; in the matter of action, the ego's position is like that of a constitutional monarch, without whose sanction no law can be passed but who hesitates long before imposing a veto on any measure put forward by Parliament.[36]

Thus we see that Freud assigns to a kind of rationality a crucial role in the health of the individual, but that what he gives with one hand he takes away with the other.

[35] Sigmund Freud, *The Ego and the Id*, p. 29.
[36] Ibid., p. 81.

Another psychiatrist, Karl Menninger, speaks of "intellection" and describes the stimulus-response process quite conventionally, then rejects it in favor of a Gestalt view but retains his S-R terminology for "convenience." Subsequently, he adds the notion of volition and of emotions and emphasizes that "the mind involves the function of the entire body and not merely the contents of the skull." This account is of interest here chiefly because, in a book influential almost three decades ago, the foregoing is the only explicit treatment of what might be called intelligence.[37]

Another widely circulated psychotherapeutic account of human behavior appears in Erich Fromm's *Escape from Freedom*, in which the pressures of conformity are seen as conspiring with the neurotic tendencies of the individual to thwart human development in the direction of responsibility and human fulfillment. Fromm sees man preferring dependence to independence. Man, in this view, is all too willing to surrender his volition to any father or mother figure who will take care of him. Carl Jung in *The Undiscovered Self* likewise ventures from a psychiatric base into an indictment of conformity that "resistance to the organized mass can be effected by the man who is as well organized in his individuality as the mass itself."[38]

These protests from some psychiatrists who see man's intelligence as overwhelmed by and surrendering to social determinants lead us naturally to a consideration of treatments of rationality by social theorists. From a large literature, I shall select for analysis the work of three theorists: George C. Homans, Peter M. Blau, and Talcott Parsons.

Homans sees man's behavior, relative to other people, as motivated in a quasi-economic fashion, wherein reward is calculated as diminished by cost to result in profit. This can scarcely be considered a serious treatment of rationality in any depth, but it does serve to indicate the social theorist's imputing of rational capacity to society's members within the long tradition

[37] Karl Menninger, *The Human Mind*, pp. 161, 164, 165.
[38] P. 60.

stretching back at least to Locke and the notion of the social contract. Thus, while most sociologists inevitably stress the social determinant of behavior, this point of view is based on the assumption that the individual is capable of a rational calculation of outcomes.

Homans, like Blau, suggests that people act to profit in an exchange. Reward, however, is a social rather than a psychological notion. Reward is thus viewed as a social constant (such as money or even food). There is no provision in these views to account for individual differences (for example, the rich man who doesn't want money and the satiated individual who doesn't consider food a reward). Also, Homans and Blau suggest that people play for a profit. Game theory provides the rules (i.e., people act in accordance with the laws of probability).[39]

Although Blau and Homans recognize the importance of individual differences and personal choice, they do not account for them. They are attempting to discuss social constants based on social agreement and conformity. These constants must be qualified on the basis of personal choice. The determination of how personal choice qualifies social constants is a job for the psychologist. Homans' and Blau's systems may "work" regardless of how we eventually explain personal choice. (Actually, Blau leaves personal choice for others to explain. Homans ties his notion of reward to reinforcement theory, which, in a sense, precludes rational choice.)

Parsons, one of the most avowedly theoretical of social theorists, has virtually nothing to say about intelligence in *The Social System*. Indeed, through most of his earlier work, nothing more venturesome about human rationality is proffered than Parsons' own background in economics would suggest—as, for instance, his treatment of "economic rationality."[40] He offers the following statement: "On the personality level . . . rational action is a type which exists within certain limits (those 'imposed by value-orientation patterns and the situation') of the organization of

[39] George C. Homans, *Social Behavior*; Peter M. Blau, *Exchange and Power in Social Life*.
[40] Talcott Parsons, *The Social System*, pp. 549–50.

the personality. On the social system level, correspondingly, there is scope for rational adjustments within certain limits imposed by the institutionalized role system."[41] Subsequently, Parsons adopted a pseudo-Freudian psychology as the individual basis for his social views, along with the following conception of behavior: "'behavior' is subject to a graded hierarchical system of control mechanisms in the cybernetic-informational theory sense, and . . . this system constitutes a continuous series extending from the highest level of the cultural and social system, through the personality and the higher-order organic systems, to organs, tissues, and cells, and indeed even to subsystems of cells."[42] Somewhat like Homans, Parsons develops an analogy between money, in society, and pleasure, in the personality. Each is a "mechanism of control—a way of imposing order on still lower-level processes."[43] Parsons is, in fact, more a "social psychologist" than Homans or Blau. He empties out the organism except for "need-dispositions." By using disposition, he makes need a social variable, and there is little accounting for personal choice. On the whole, as the foregoing quotations suggest, we need not expect much help from sociology in our attempt to cope with the problem of explaining human rationality.

My position approaches that of the philosopher George H. Mead, who—more than a generation ago—was speaking of "reflective thought" (similar to my "deliberation").

The intelligent man as distinguished from the intelligent animal presents to himself what is going to happen. . . . it is this picture . . . of what the future is to be as determining our present conduct that is the characteristic of human intelligence—the future as present in terms of ideas. . . . There is some sort of a problem before us, and our statement of the problem is in terms of a future situation which will enable us to meet it by our present reactions. . . . The man who acts, as we say, rationally . . . identifies "this as leading to that" . . . so as to make possible the control of conduct with

---

[41] Ibid., p. 549.
[42] Talcott Parsons, *Social Structure and Personality*, p. 114.
[43] Ibid., p. 125.

reference to it. . . . [This] is the distinctive thing in human intelligence which is not found in animal intelligence.[44]

I would not make the distinction so sharply as Mead does, saying, rather, that as we go up the phylogenetic scale, prediction becomes more of a long-term affair. The discontinuity between higher animals and man is not one I can totally endorse; when a rabbit jumps he expects to land.

Mead, describing himself as a "social behaviorist," preserves the stimulus-response connection with great subtlety, deriving the variety and adaptability of response from the possibility of "pick[ing] out responses which are there in other reactions and put[ting] them together. . . . The psychology of attention," he tells us, "ousted the psychology of association. . . . Voluntary attention . . . makes possible the isolation and recombination of responses."[45] He continues: "Now, where does this thought process itself take place? If you like, I am here sidestepping the question as to just what is going on in the area of the brain . . . identified with consciousness. . . . Consciousness is functional, not substantive. . . . What is located, what does take place in the brain . . . is the physiological process whereby we lose and regain consciousness; a process which is somewhat analogous to that of pulling down and raising a window shade."[46] Mead's extended treatment of the individual parallels in several respects the theory I am presenting, and, indeed, I hope that the following psychological elaborations of that theory will expand and clarify some of Mead's suggestions about rationality. Although his emphasis on the "social" is much broader, his account of mental operation in the individual seems in some ways comparable. His propositions, however, appear to be offered as a sort of philosophical observation, whereas the theoretical account I have outlined in this book attempts a systematic explanation of man's rationality and its influences. Philosophers such as Dewey and Mead provide scattered and provocative insight concerning

[44] George H. Mead, *Mind, Self, and Society*, pp. 119–20.
[45] Ibid., pp. 95–96.
[46] Ibid., p. 112.

human rationality. What is offered here, by contrast, is an extended and sequenced account of how rationality develops and operates. Thus, I have attempted to construct the basis for a set of interrelated propositions that can be empirically tested.

Although I believe that mental process will eventually be explained in neurophysiological terms, I am not interested in taking a stand on the neurophysiological correlates of the process I am describing. For example, the term *memories* is used here to denote mental representations of events. A memory can be used validly as a psychological construct, whether or not it corresponds to present neurophysiological definitions such as "cell assembly" and "phase sequence." On the other hand, I believe that my approach is consistent with the work done by exponents of the "cell-assembly" school, such as Hebb and Milner.

Indeed, I would hope that, in suggesting phenomena to be explained and in opening avenues of inquiry, my work may be as helpful to neurologists as their work has been to me. My interest is much broader than the study of brain function, however. I am concerned with the relationship between thought and action as the individual attempts to cope with the environment. Thus, this focus may have heuristic value for neurology as well as for other approaches to the understanding of behavior.

PART II / THE THEORY

3

PREDICTION

Theories provide a dynamic account of behavior; descriptions do not. Descriptions account only for the behavior that occurs. Theories attempt to explain why the behavior occurs as it does. Thus, a theory must attempt to account for the underlying forces that impel behavior.

To explain the dynamics of behavior, a theory need not be concerned with the source of the energy that activates those underlying forces, for all living things have energy and are active. The issue that must be of concern is the direction in which behavior is impelled by these forces—that is, why individuals behave in one way rather than another.[1]

In order to explain the direction of behavior, it is necessary to identify a basic motive that directs behavior. Such a motive then becomes an underlying assumption upon which the theory is based, and accounts of behavior are regarded as attempts to fulfill the basic motive. From the viewpoint of this theory, there is a fundamental overriding and pervasive motive that gives impetus and direction to behavior. In short, *individuals are inherently motivated to predict their relationship with the environment. This impels them to develop their ability to predict through learning.*

Prediction is the mind's contribution to adaptation. All indi-

[1] A scientific "theory" will be restricted here to mean an explanation of why events occur as they do. Descriptions or models of how events occur— that is, simple analogies—are not considered theories.

42

viduals must maintain a predictable relationship with the environment in order to adapt. When an infant cries to his mother for food, he predicts it will come. When a young child walks to school, he predicts that a certain route will lead him there. Without the ability to predict what may happen, the individual is disoriented and cannot understand or deal with his environment.

The notion that individuals make predictions has been held and contemplated for many years. However, in the literature, much of the work related to prediction has been conducted under the heading of expectancy. E. C. Tolman was responsible for gaining theoretical legitimacy for expectancy. In essence, Tolman contends that if two stimuli are paired, expectancy is the situation in which the individual behaves in the presence of stimulus one as if stimulus two will be present. Tolman goes on to elaborate this oversimplified version of his formulation of how expectancy is produced.

Others also have stressed the importance of expectancy in accounting for behavior. Ccoige Kelly viewed man as an "incipient scientist," seeking "to predict, and thus control, the course of events." In Kelly's theory of personality, "anticipation" is regarded as a fundamental postulate: "A person's processes are psychologically channelized by the ways in which he anticipates events." In explaining the phrase "anticipates events," Kelly states: "Like the prototype of the scientist that he is, man seeks prediction. His structured network of pathways leads towards the future so that he may anticipate it. Man ultimately seeks to anticipate real events."[2]

Robert C. Bolles has proposed the following primary law of learning: "What is learned is that certain events, cues (S), predict certain other, biologically important events, consequences (S*). An animal may incidentally show new responses, but what it learns is an expectancy that represents and corresponds to the S–S* contingency."[3] Some animals, according to Bolles, are able to appreciate new environmental contingencies. In other words, their behavior is mainly a function of their expectations.

[2] George A. Kelly, *The Psychology of Personal Constructs*, pp. 46, 49.
[3] Robert C. Bolles, "Reinforcement, Expectancy and Learning," p. 402.

THE THEORY

William K. Estes uses the word *anticipation* to explain human behavior that does not fit neatly into the animal-laboratory-oriented reward/punishment model. Estes maintains that in the "case of a normal human learner a reward does not necessarily strengthen, nor a punishment weaken, the response which produces it. . . . In any choice situation the individual is assumed actively to scan the available alternatives and to be guided to a choice by feedback from anticipated rewards."[4]

There have also been a number of studies of molar behavior that have given credence to Tolman's statement about expectancy.

One of the earliest and most striking observations of reward expectancy was that of Tinklepaugh (1956). In his experiment, food was placed under one of two containers while the monkey was looking but prevented from immediate access to the cans of food. Later the monkey was permitted to choose between the containers and showed skill in choosing correctly. The behavior which is pertinent here occurred when, after a banana had been hidden under one of the cups, the experimenter substituted for it a lettuce leaf (a less preferred food). The monkey rejected the lettuce leaf and engaged in definite searching behavior. Somewhat the same sort of behavior was found by Elliot (1956) when the food in the goal box of a rat maze experiment was changed from bran mash to sunflower seed. More systematic experiments have been carried out since with chimpanzees (Cowles and Nissen, 1956). There is little doubt that animals have some sort of precognition or expectancy of goal objects.[5]

More recent research related to brain function is giving increasing credibility to the notion of expectancy. It has been shown that the components of responses evoked by visual stimuli vary with the expectation of the organism.[6] Moreover, the work of E. N. Sokolov suggests that environmental input is matched against a neuronal model that represents an expectancy of the organism.

[4] William K. Estes, "Reinforcement in Human Behavior," p. 729.
[5] Ernest R. Hilgard, *Theories of Learning*, p. 192.
[6] Samuel Sutton, Patricia Tueting, and E. R. John, "Information Delivery"; Manfred Haider, Paul Spong, and Donald B. Lindsley, "Cortical Evoked Potential in Humans."

So it appears that expectancy is an established facet of mental process that has been gaining credibility as more evidence is obtained with the passage of time. The implication that is added from the perspective of the present theory is the assumption that prediction is a basic motive that directs behavior.

As was stated earlier, the theory will focus on rational determinants of behavior. Prediction as the force that directs behavior imputes a rational function to the mind. In other words, the individual is behaving rationally when he is attempting to test the predictions generated by his mind. For example, the child is behaving rationally when he follows the route that he predicts will lead him to school. Thus, in this context, the formulation and testing of predictions against environmental events is rational behavior.

This theory will attempt to explain behavior that is particularly human—behavior that transcends the accomplishments of lower forms of life. It is in the ability to predict that man seems to excel other forms of life. Man shares the ability to predict the consequences of simpler psychomotor actions with infrahumans. But man's ability to calculate statistically the probability of landing on the moon, in a given amount of time, in a prescribed way, is evidence of his ability to excel in forecasting. In fact, man's ability to use his powers of prediction to discover and invent new phenomena represents the acme of his predictive ability.

Other motives have been assumed to explain the forces that direct man's behavior. Some of these are tension reduction, homeostasis, self-actualization, and the lust for pleasure. Although the assumption of each of these motives has aided our understanding of behavior, each has led us to focus more on the accomplishments that man shares with other creatures. They do not contribute to the understanding of man's ability to make complicated and far-reaching predictions and to work actively to fulfill the predictions.

When tension reduction is the basic motive impelling the individual, he is seen as being in a state of tension from which he is persistently attempting to recover. The individual is portrayed as being victimized by the onslaught of the environment

THE THEORY

and directing his energies to overcome the tension these encounters induce. From this perspective, the individual is viewed as the reactor to externally imposed forces that produce tension in him. It is true that man, like other creatures, is victimized by the environment, but this point of view by no means focuses on the excellence of man, who can, through prediction, prevent the environment from victimizing him.

Tension reduction appears to be most closely related to the motives that govern the behavior of very young children and immature adults. It suggests a paucity of the intellectual equipment needed to make predictions in coping with the environment. The child and the inept adult spend a major portion of their time attempting to recover from the onslaughts of unmanageable external forces.

It is no wonder, then, that tension reduction is often the motive associated with pathological behavior. Such behavior can be thought of as directed at overcoming a deficit, an infirmity. The deficit may be emotional. For instance, it may be related to the compensatory behavior of a thirty-year-old adult who, let us say, is five years of age emotionally. The behavior of such a thirty-year-old adult would include attempts to overcome the twenty-five-year deficit between his chronological age and his emotional age in order to reduce tension. Or an individual might have an intellectual deficit, which he would try constantly to overcome. In this case, too, the individual is not at the maturational level of his chronological peers. Thus, tension reduction seems to be the motive of persons engaged in behavior directed at overcoming some deficit.

When homeostasis is the basic motive of an individual, he seeks to establish and maintain equilibrium. As tension is induced by the environment, countervailing forces begin to operate within him to reinstate equilibrium. Thus, homeostasis suggests slightly more than tension reduction, for the individual reacts to the environment, when it begins to induce tension, so as to prevent the state of tension from becoming too pronounced. But this focus still regards the individual as a passive reactor to the environment.

Prediction

Self-actualization as a motive impels the individual toward more than the reduction of tension and the maintenance of equilibrium. In addition to reacting to the environment, the individual is struggling to emerge into something more tomorrow than he is today—he is seeking to fulfill his potential or to self-actualize through the pursuit of goals.

At first glance, it may seem that self-actualization points to a function in which man excels. But this is not necessarily so, for self-actualization may be interpreted to imply merely that the individual is impelled to grow, and the growth process is something man shares with all living creatures, even plants. All creatures grow, in spite of their tensions and imbalances. Growth hardly characterizes man's outstanding accomplishments. There may be goals more exalted than growth that may be attributed to the motive of self-actualization. However, the implications of self-actualization are vague and amorphous. It is difficult to determine the goals that one is pursuing when he is self-actualizing. Actually, self-actualization might be subsumed under the prediction motive if we were to contend that an individual is self-actualizing when he is attempting to improve his ability to predict.

Finally, we need to consider the popular pleasure-pain principle as a motive. This postulate, which asserts that individuals seek pleasure and avoid pain, was advocated by Freud and adopted by many other theorists. The pleasure-pain principle is often tied in with tension reduction and homeostasis because when pain is induced the individual is in a state of tension or disequilibrium. But the assumption presents its own distinct problems. One might ask, for example, why individuals who are supposed to seek pleasure watch horror movies. Does it give them pleasure to be frightened? And then there is the problem of dealing with masochism from this particular theoretical point of view. Does a masochist seek to have pain inflicted upon him because it gives him pleasure? To say the least, these questions introduce anomalies, which perhaps can be reconciled within the framework of particular theories but nevertheless cast some doubt upon the pleasure-pain principle as the prime motive of individuals.

The Theory

Moreover, the most pleasure-giving alternative is not always preferred and pursued. It is not pursued if its achievement cannot be predicted. Something less pleasurable but more readily attainable may be preferred.

From the present theoretical position it can be contended that in a certain sense and under certain circumstances individuals will seek painful experiences. An individual who has suffered a painful encounter will tend to avoid a similar encounter in the future. However, his propensity to predict may challenge him to conceive of a means of dealing with the problem. If he conceives of a way of coping with the painful experience, he may seek another encounter with it to test the new predictions he has formulated. For example, a young boy who has been defeated in a fight with a peer will tend to avoid the peer. But he will be interested in finding a way of dealing with the peer in the future. If he discovers a way which he predicts will lead to a victory, he may seek another bout with the peer to test the prediction.

Prediction can be seen as a motive more basic than pleasure when one considers that the individual must maintain a predictable relationship with the environment to obtain his needs and desires, whatever they may be. The maintenance of predictability is superordinate to the pursuit of one's preferences because it is prerequisite to achieving that which is preferred. When the maintenance of predictability is seriously threatened, the individual will forsake his immediate preference in order to maintain a predictable relationship with the environment. In short, the individual is motivated to predict his relationship with the environment. This impels him to develop his ability to predict. And it is the ability to predict that enables him to reduce tension, maintain homeostasis, self-actualize, and obtain pleasure.

Reinforcement is another predominant force that is said to shape behavior. However, reinforcement is more correctly viewed as an incentive provided from the environment rather than a motive of the individual. In most reinforcement studies, desire is created by withholding food from the organism until it becomes very hungry. From this point of view, the motive of the

49

organism is hunger. When the individuals in a study of reinforcement are starved, hunger acts as a constant influence on
behavior. As different forms of reinforcement are then tested on
the individuals and differential behavior results, the results are
interpreted to be a function of the different reinforcement treatments, rather than of hunger. The question arises, Would the
same results be achieved if the individuals were not motivated
by hunger? Could it be that the reason reinforcement does not
work as well on humans as on infrahumans is that we do not
starve humans to develop comparable motivation and that we
have not been able to find another general motive that can be
reinforced to shape behavior?

This controversy cannot be settled here, but it does provide a
basis for relating reinforcement to the prediction motive. The
individual is reinforced when a prediction is confirmed, as will
be seen in chapter 13, when learning is considered.

In summary, the theory proposed here posits that the individual is motivated to predict his relationship with the environment. This impels him to develop his ability to predict through
learning and to extend his scope of prediction whenever possible. Ever extending attempts to conceive and validate predictions
against events leads to an increasing mastery of the environment.
Although there is nothing new in emphasizing prediction as an
important facet of behavior, the proposed theory is distinct in
that it posits prediction as a basic motive and describes mental
process and behavior as organizing to fulfill this motive.

4

The Structure of the Mind

There is a need to establish a basic structural unit that represents a record of the information stored in the mind and that guides the behavior of the individual. The term *neuroprint* is selected for this purpose. A *neuroprint is the mental representation of a set of relationships among stimuli.*

In neurological terms, a neuroprint is a coding within the brain of the relationships among events, which does not necessarily imply a corresponding neural growth of the brain. Current evidence indicates that such codings do occur, although the process through which they take place is still subject to considerable speculation.

Prediction is based on the knowledge of relationships. If one event is related to another, it is possible to predict one event from the other. Because neuroprints are mental representations of the relationship of events, they provide the individual with the means of making predictions.

Neuroprints may function in two primary ways. They can be represented by ideas that make the individual aware of the relationship among events and the predictions he is able to make about the events. Or they can define mental programs that direct the behavior of the individual and enable him to predict that certain activities will lead to specified outcomes. Thus, neuroprints may be represented by ideas, programs, or both. The sum total of our ideas and programs represents our store of knowledge —the information we have stored in our minds.

THE STRUCTURE OF THE MIND

An idea is a function of a neuroprint that represents a mental image of the relationship among stimuli.

Neuroprints generate the ideas we have about ourselves and about the world. The ideas we have represent our understanding of the relationship among events, the composition of our bodies and of the environment, and the way in which we may interact with the environment. Ideas represent our awareness of the predictions we may make, because, if we are aware that one event is related to another, it is possible to predict one event from the other. Ideas permit us to be aware of events and how we feel about the events.

As a man drives to his office, he is aware of the road before him and the scenery he is passing, as well as of the traffic problems confronting him at the moment. In addition, he is aware of more than he sees. He knows there is a back seat behind him, and perhaps a package on the seat. Moreover, as he travels, his mind may wander to an experience he had playing with his child the previous evening or to the work he must accomplish when he arrives at the office. Thus, ideas represent the awareness one has about what is happening, what has happened, or what may happen.

Ideas include also one's feelings about his experiences—that is, ideas include the value he places upon the events he experiences. As a man proceeds to his office, he is aware not only of what is happening but also of the feelings he has about the events. As he views the scenery along the road, he is aware not only of its composition but also of the way it makes him feel—of his reactions to its beauty or its ugliness. If he should be threatened by an oncoming car, he might be frightened by it, or if he should reminisce about his child, a feeling of pleasure may come over him. A person's feelings about his experiences represent the way in which he values the experiences.

When ideas are vivid and detailed, the individual has a keen awareness of the experience that the idea represents. However, some ideas represent faint impressions of experiences. In many such cases, the individual may be aware of his feelings but only vaguely aware of the event associated with his feelings.

A program is the function of a neuroprint that can control the order in which a sequence of procedures is performed leading through a series of predicted outcomes. Programs guide the behavior of the individual. Each program represents a sequence of activities that lead to specified outcomes, and each subroutine of a program represents a single activity that leads to a specific outcome. When a program is being executed, it controls the sequence of operations the individual is performing. The individual anticipates or predicts that the operations will lead to the events specified in the program.

The terms *program* and *subroutine* are used to denote the mental apparatus that guides behavior because there is a close resemblance between our definitions of the terms and the understanding of the terms that have been developed in computer language. The main difference between the term *program* as it is used in computer language and in this theoretical context is that computer programs tend to operate on the basis of content alone. Mental programs involve both the content of events and the feelings associated with the content or, more specifically, the content and arousal functions.

Certain programs guide the actions of the individual. Some of these programs operate without the individual's awareness for the most part. For example, the programs guiding autonomic functions of the body such as breathing usually operate without one's awareness. Other programs, such as those that guide a person from one room of his home to another, operate on a more conscious level. In addition to programs that guide motor activities, there are programs that process information. These programs are organized to accept information and store it so that it may be retrieved to improve prediction in the future. For example, the dictionary and the white pages of the telephone directory are programmed alphabetically. The yellow pages of the directory are programmed according to the services and products offered. Books are stored and retrieved in the library according to an information-processing program.

The predictions prescribed by the program being executed are confirmed when sensory feedback indicates that events are occurring as predicted. In other words, confirmation of predictions is achieved when there is a match between events and the predictions prescribed by the program being executed. When that match occurs, there is confirmation that the individual is maintaining a predictable relationship with the environment. On the other hand, if there is a mismatch between the events and the program being executed, the individual is alerted and consequently attempts to restore predictability.

There are, therefore, two kinds of programs: programs that guide action and programs that process information. The latter type includes programs that match sensory events with the programs that are currently guiding behavior to determine whether events are occurring as predicted. The matching process will be elaborated upon in the discussion on the dynamics of behavior.

Since both ideas and programs are functions of neuroprints, they are closely related. The programs of which the individual is aware form some of the ideas he has about himself and his world. His awareness of the programs he can execute represents his understanding of the behavior he can perform and the outcomes he can predict as a consequence of his behavior. Thus, programs are a part of one's ideas. Moreover, ideas are incorporated into programs. Ideas lead to the formulation of programs, because one's awareness of the relationship between events can be used in the formulation of a program to pursue a desired event.

Ideas are modified through the execution of programs. Programs guide behavior toward predicted outcomes. When variations from the predicted outcomes are observed, ideas are changed in accordance with the observed variations. Programs are modified on the basis of information drawn from ideas. The understanding of a new relationship between events is a basis for conceiving new programs. Furthermore, it can be the idea of an experience that triggers the selection of a program to guide behavior. An idea prescribes a valued outcome to be pursued, which in turn initiates the selection of a program that prescribes procedures predicted to lead to the valued outcome.

Both ideas and programs are expressions of neuroprints and cannot be dichotomized as independent processes. In addition, many ideas may be projected which, at the moment, do not have

programmatic implications. For instance, daydreams about a pleasant retreat in the country may not serve to control any of the operations of the individual toward predicted outcomes at the time. Also, there are many programs, such as those governing the autonomic functions of the body, that do not yield ideational material. To complete the discussion of mental structure, let us consider how neuroprints develop and are organized so that they may be retrieved to facilitate prediction.

There are three levels of neuroprint development. Proceeding from the more primitive to the higher levels, they are instincts, memories, and abstractions.

Instincts are inherited neuroprints. The individual is born with an inventory of neuroprints, which we may refer to as instincts. Instincts define programs. They do not produce ideas. The programs defined by instincts are executed involuntarily and automatically.

Many of the instinctive programs are reflexes. Reflexes are inflexible instinctive programs. An inflexible program is one that is executed in a fixed order. Most of the autonomic functions of the body present at birth are controlled by reflexive programs. For example, the program that controls the respiratory process is instinctive and inflexible. It is inherited. It operates involuntarily and automatically. Moreover, the breathing program is inflexible in that inhaling and exhaling proceed in a fixed sequence.

In addition to the inventory of reflexive programs that are inherited, there are other programs that provide some small degree of flexibility in their operation. These programs are often referred to as tropisms. For example, the nest-building instinct of birds is a tropism. It permits some flexibility in the way in which the bird may interact with the environment to obtain the material it needs to build its nest. The sex instinct is also a tropism, for it permits some flexibility in the way it is expressed and in the objects that may be selected for sexual expression.

Although ideas are produced through the observation and learning of events, instincts do influence the formation of ideas when learning occurs. For example, the ideas that one learns concerning desirable sex objects are influenced by one's sex instincts. There is

an instinctual tendency to choose a sex object of the same species.

A *servoprogram is a reflexive program that governs the adjustment of events and neuroprints to gain a match between them.* The notion of a servoprogram is adopted from the term *servomechanism.* Servomechanisms sense information and make performance adjustments according to a criterion. A thermostat is an example of a servomechanism. It senses temperature changes and turns the heat on and off to maintain the criterion level of temperature at which the thermostat is set.

Servoprograms control the matching functions of behavior. The general criterion against which a servoprogram operates is toward the maintenance of a predictable relationship with the environment, so that when an unpredictable event emerges, adjustments are made to the neuroprints stored in the mind and to events in order to promote prediction. Servoprograms are part of the individual's instinctual perceptual equipment. By contributing to the modification of neuroprints and events to improve prediction they are an indispensable part of the learning process.

Memories represent the second level of neuroprint development. A *memory may be defined as a neuroprint representing the relationship among events that have been observed directly.* Memories are formed through observation and are learned. Instincts provide the basic inventory of neuroprints. Memories add to and modify these inherited neuroprints; they do not replace instincts.

Inherited neuroprints delimit one's potential. Experience determines the extent to which one may develop to his potential. It is as if the inherited neuroprints represented keys seeking locks to fit and experience provided the opportunities for the keys to find locks. For example, the sex drive is an instinct that develops and seeks the opportunity for expression. Experience provides the opportunity for the individual to express the instinct by providing sex objects.

As the infant becomes aware of his surroundings, his experiences result in the formation of memories in the following manner. Continued exposure to a sensory event results in a change in the mental state of the individual; this change may be described as the development of a memory of the event. Thereafter, the appearance of the event will result in the automatic matching, for similarities and differences, of the event to the neuroprints stored in the mind. A similarity between the event and the memory of the event will result in the elicitation of the memory. Elicitation of the memory causes the event to be recognized as familiar. For instance, when an individual is repeatedly exposed to an object such as a ball, a memory of the ball will form in his mind. Subsequently, when he sees a ball, it will be automatically matched for similarities and differences with the various neuroprints stored in his mind. Because the ball matches more closely the memory of a ball than other memories, the memory of the ball will be elicited. This results in the object being recognized as a ball. In short, memories represent ideas of events that have been observed in the past.

The programs that are learned become part of the individual's memories of the events he experiences. The individual memorizes programs when he learns that a certain sequence of operations leads to particular outcomes. He may then attempt to control the sequence of operations to produce the outcomes.

As the infant matures and is able to take note of his surroundings, his instinctive programs become extended and modified as a result of his experience. For example, the sucking response, which is governed by an instinctive program, becomes extended and modified. The primitive program that guides the sucking response is modified to accommodate the sucking of milk from a bottle.

Learned programs that operate inflexibly are generally thought of as habits. Although habits initially are based on instinctive programs, they are a product of learning and soon develop a character of their own. For instance, drinking may be based on sucking, but it is learned and distinct from sucking. In many cases habits are substituted for instinctive programs. The habit of drinking milk from a glass is eventually substituted for the sucking of milk from a bottle. As the infant matures into childhood, he learns habits from experience as a result of instruction. Recognition may be a form of habit. The association between a sensory event and a neuroprint in the mind that causes the individual to recognize the sensory event occurs in a fixed or inflexible manner.

THE STRUCTURE OF THE MIND

Flexible programs form as the individual learns alternative ways of behaving. A flexible program is a program in which the operations controlled by the program may be performed in more than one order. An example of a flexible program would be a program for completing the purchases prescribed by a shopping list. The items on the list could be acquired in any order without interfering with the execution of the program. Of course, programs may prescribe various degrees of flexibility with respect to the kinds of behavior they control.

To contrast a habit with a flexible program, we can use the example of driving a car. Shifting gears is directed by habit, because the tasks involved need to be performed in a fixed manner. On the other hand, tasks such as adjusting the seat before driving the car and turning on the lights and windshield wipers can occur in any order.

Abstractions represent the third level of neuroprint development. *An abstraction is a neuroprint representing a category of related memories.* As an individual is exposed to a new sensory event, and as a memory of the event is being formed, the sensory event is automatically compared with existing memories for similarities and differences so that it might be predicted. In addition, when a memory of the sensory event is formed, it is compared with other memories and categorized with similar memories as part of the storage process. The categorization of similar memories forms abstractions.

In the process of categorization the individual recognizes an event as a special case within a general category of events. An abstraction is not created directly by a sensory stimulation but by the categorization of memories that have been associated as having something in common. An apple is a sensory object represented in the mind by a memory. The term *vegetable* is an abstraction representing a category of memories of items similar to apples. *An abstraction cannot be experienced directly as a sensory event, although it is inferred from sensory experience.* In other words, a memory represents a sensory event; an abstraction represents not a sensory event but, rather, a category of similar memories.

THE THEORY

The process of abstraction does not end with the formation of memories into categories. Once categories have been formed, they can be compared for similarities and differences, and this leads to the formation of higher-level abstractions. For example, vegetables and meats, which are both abstractions, may be classified together within the category "food" as parts of a higher-level abstraction.

Abstractions, therefore, permit the individual to have ideas about the similarities and differences among events and objects. From these ideas, he is able to understand alternatives, which is the basis for making choices. For example, if he understands that food will satisfy his hunger, he can select from among the many food items available to satisfy his hunger.

Moreover, programs may be categorized together to form an abstraction. This may mean that the programs in a category share in common their ability to control some of the same operations. Therefore, one program in the category might be substituted for another. For example, programs that govern the acquisition of food may form an abstraction. This provides the basis for selecting alternative procedures to obtain food. Abstractions also have other functions, which shall be described in chapter 7.

Abstractions produce ideas about categories of events. These ideas represent an image of the features that the items in a category share in common. For example, one may have an idea of the abstraction "people" as a general representation of the features that people share in common. In one individual's mind, the idea might represent a general outline or shadow of the features of people.

Ideas, then, may be represented by memories or abstractions. When an idea of an event is elicited, the event to which the idea corresponds is recognized as familiar. When an idea is produced by a memory, the corresponding event is recognized as familiar because it is related to a specific event in the individual's past experience. When an idea is produced by an abstraction, the corresponding event is recognized as familiar to some extent, in a general way—that is, the individual recognizes some of the features of the event as familiar. When a memory produces an idea, the event to which the memory corresponds will be familiar in greater

The Structure of the Mind

detail than when an abstraction produces an idea of an event. For this reason, memories provide a basis for a greater degree of familiarity than do abstractions.

The foregoing description of the structure of the mind may be summarized as follows. Neuroprints are the basic structural units of the mind. Their two primary functions are representation of ideas and prescription of programs. Neuroprints develop at three levels. Proceeding from the more primitive to the higher levels of organization, these are instincts, memories, and abstractions. The higher levels of organization are extensions of the lower levels. Ideas and programs were discussed for each of the three levels. In general, as neuroprints develop from level to level, the individual's ability to predict improves. (See chapter 8 for a discussion of neuroprint hierarchies.)

The attempt to describe the mental representation of events by defining terms such as *neuroprint* is not new. Tolman introduced the phrase *cognitive map* for the purpose and Piaget the term *schema*. Hebb, in attempting to tie the mental representation of events to neurophysiology, introduced the terms *cell assembly* and *phase sequence* for the same purpose. Nor is it new to conceive of prediction as a capability of the mind. Tolman's theory deals at length with the way in which one's cognitive maps establish an anticipation of things to come. However, I am introducing the term *neuroprint* to prevent other theoretical perspectives from interfering with the understanding of the theory presented in this book. What appears to be somewhat distinctive about this theoretical position is the positing of prediction as a basic motive of individuals and the description of mental activity organizing and operating to fulfill this motive.

5

The Dynamics of Behavior: Matching

From the discussion of the structure of the mind, let us proceed to consider the way in which the mind functions. This requires more than a description of the operation of the mind itself. It requires a description of the way the mind operates in conjunction with the events it is attempting to predict. For this reason we will be concerned in this chapter with the dynamics of behavior, which includes the relationship between mental function and events.

It was said that programs prescribe a sequence of procedures that lead to a series of predicted events, and that each procedure may be regarded as a subroutine of the program. When a program is selected and executed, it guides behavior, and the sequence of events that ensue are tested to determine whether they are occurring as predicted. This requires a matching, for correspondence, of the selected program with the events that actually occur. If there is a match, the efficacy of the program is confirmed and the experience confirms the individual's ability to predict his relationship with the environment. Thus, there is a continuing attempt to match programs with happenings. The matching process, although more complex than has been indicated so far, is the essence of the dynamics of behavior. The individual is continually matching events with prevailing programs for the confirmation of predictions.

Servoprograms govern all aspects of the matching process to gain a match between neuroprints and events so that the indi-

The Dynamics of Behavior

vidual may maintain a predictable relationship with the environment. Programs are adjusted to match events, and events are adjusted to match programs, in order to attain predictability. For example, an individual building a model airplane might assemble existing materials according to the blueprint. Or he might modify the material, the plan, or both to gain a match between them in the construction of the plane.

In matching events with neuroprints, the individual seeks an optimum degree of predictability. When there is too little predictability, he avoids novelty and seeks situations that he has predicted in the past, in order to gain a closer match between events and neuroprints. When there is too much predictability, he is bored and seeks to extend his ability to predict by seeking novelty.

It is when there is too much predictability and novelty is sought that discoveries are most likely to be made. And, as I have said, it is man's propensity to discover that contributes heavily to his excellence. Man has found the means of predicting his subsistence and the gratification of his appetites to a much greater degree than other creatures. Thus, man will tend to become bored more readily and seek new worlds to conquer. Let us consider the mental functions that are related to predictability.

How does environmental input stimulate mental activity? Events stimulate at least two functions of the mind—the content function, which interprets the specific nature or content of the event, and the arousal function, which is a nonspecific, diffuse function that generates a degree of arousal or feeling that the individual associates with the event.[1]

The degree of arousal that is associated with an event is correlated with the intensity of feeling and disturbance the event

[1] According to Pribram ("Emotion," p. 12), each interaction between environment and organism involves at least two components: (1) discrete interaction by way of the brain's sensory mode, its specific, classical projection systems, and its core homeostats; and (2) a "nonspecific," relatively diffuse interaction by way of reticular and related formations. These nonspecific systems act as a bias on the specific reactions; the set point or value toward which a specific interaction tends to stabilize is set by the "nonspecific activity."

elicits when it intrudes. The more excessive the arousal, the more disturbed, excited, and vigilant the individual will become when the event occurs.

The notion of arousal and its function was adopted from activation theory. This is how activation was described by Malmo: "The neuropsychological dimension of activation may be briefly described as follows. The continuum extending from deep sleep at the low activation end to 'excited' states at the high activation end is a function of the amount of cortical bombardment by the ARAS (Ascending Reticular Activating System of the brain) such that the greater the cortical bombardment the higher the activation."[2] The term *arousal* is intended to denote the same process as activation. However, I prefer to use *arousal* rather than *activation* to convey the meaning proposed in my theory because arousal implies an intensity of feeling that activation does not seem to imply. The basic characteristics of arousal will be introduced in this chapter, but its major functions will be presented in chapter 10, where emotion is discussed. In essence, arousal is considered to be a component of emotion closely associated with the survival instincts.

Arousal may be generated when there is either too much or too little predictability. When there is too much predictability, arousal will increase, signifying a felt state of boredom and a desire to seek novelty and adventure. Boredom is, therefore, an aroused state of mind. Too little predictability will also increase arousal. A prolonged and marked mismatch between events and neuroprints generates excessive arousal and signifies a situation in which the environment is alien and confusing. Thus, the individual seeks an optimum degree of predictability. The extent to which events are predictable determines the degree of arousal that is generated, and the urgency and value of making a prediction is reflected in the degree of arousal that is felt.

The contention that too little predictability generates arousal is discussed by Bindra in his book entitled *Motivation*.[3] The contention that too much predictability or boredom generates arousal

[2] Robert B. Malmo, "Activation," p. 384.
[3] Pp. 229–35.

is supported by the research of London and Schubert. They found that boredom increases autonomic arousal as measured by galvanic skin potential, skin conductance, and heart rate. They also state that "stimulation which is redundant for the individual . . . produces increased arousal. At the other end of the continuum rapidly changing [novel] stimulation also causes increased arousal. Thus, autonomic arousal seems to reach a minimum at some intermediate level of stimulus change."[4]

Excessive arousal is associated with mental instability, which in turn interferes with the individual's ability to predict and negotiate the environment. In such a state the individual's ability to maintain a predictable relationship with the environment becomes tenuous. The ability and interest to formulate and confirm a prediction is associated with a moderate-to-high degree of arousal. Finally, a disinterest in predicting is related to a low degree of arousal, which represents a relaxed or resting state.

Mental instability is the state of mind in which the individual is unable to predict the environment. As a result, the individual becomes excessively aroused. Mental instability is generated by the inability to confirm predictions against environmental events.

It should be noted that a prediction may be confirmed through an encounter with the environment or through an autistic mode. Autism is an idea and/or program that operates divorced from environmental events. For example, it may be predicted that the acquisition of food will reduce a baby's hunger, or it may be predicted that his hunger will be reduced, at least temporarily, if he sucks his thumb. Autism gives the illusion of the confirmation of a prediction. In the above example of the baby sucking his thumb, he has the illusion of reduced hunger because he associates the reduction of hunger with having things in his mouth. Mental activity is regulated to confirm predictions, and the conception and confirmation of predictions will reduce arousal whether the predictions are confirmed through interaction with the environment or through an autistic mode of behavior.

Formulation and confirmation of predictions are related not

[4] Harvey London and Daniel S. P. Schubert, "Increase of Autonomic Arousal by Boredom," p. 33.

only to the arousal function; they are associated with the content function as well. Predictions are based on the content of an event. The content function defines the specific composition of an event so that the event may be identified and predicted. For example, a rise in air temperature and its accompanying sensation of heat may arise from different environmental sources. The content function enables the individual to distinguish the sun from a fire or a radiator as a source of heat.

The content of an event generates impressions of its structural and functional composition—for example, sound is transmitted in waves. Thus, the content of an event emanates from the event itself and is conveyed to the individual as stimulation. Although each individual can gain an idiosyncratic impression of an event, many events can be defined objectively in terms of their content. Conversely, arousal is an internal reaction that occurs upon the reception of a stimulation. The reception of a stimulation generates an arousal reaction that results in an intensity of feeling assigned to the event by the individual. Since arousal emanates from within the individual, the arousal associated with an event tends to be more subjective than impressions of the content of an event.

To restate: Too much or too little predictability generates arousal. Arousal, in turn, indicates the degree of felt value of conceiving and confirming a prediction. On the other hand, it is the content function that defines the basis for conceiving and confirming predictions. For example, it would be the content function that distinguishes the demand to predict the reduction of hunger from the demand to predict the reduction of thirst. For this reason, when arousal becomes excessive but the content of the idea that is associated with the arousal is not well enough defined, the individual's ability to predict the reduction of the arousal is seriously impaired. He is aroused, but without having the "foggiest idea" of what to do about it. He finds himself in an undefined state of free-floating arousal.

The arousal and content functions appear to combine in influencing the formation of neuroprints, so that when a neuroprint forms it represents both the content of an event and the degree of arousal that was associated with the event. Once a neuroprint has formed, the ideas it may generate project the content of the event the neuroprint represents plus the feelings or emotion the individual has about the event. However, in the projection of an idea, content and arousal seem to become blended, and not only do the individual's feelings about the event project an intensity of feeling or arousal, but also the intensity of feeling is defined specifically by the content of the idea. As a result, the individual's feelings are projected in terms of their intensity about a specific event.

The basic unit of analysis for assessing the relationship between events and mental activity is the feedback loop. Because each program includes a series of predictions (which are defined by the subroutines of the program), each prediction must be tested against sensory feedback to determine whether events are proceeding as prescribed by the program. The testing of each individual prediction in a program against sensory feedback defines a feedback loop. It is the basic unit for analyzing the testing of predictions.

As a program proceeds to guide behavior, a series of feedback loops is completed to test the predictions in the program—to determine whether the individual is on the "right track." For example, the route to a man's office is a program that he follows to get there. The program includes predictions of many milestones he expects to pass on the way. As he passes each milestone en route, a feedback loop is completed. If there is correspondence between sensory feedback and the program depicting the route, he continues to follow the dictates of the program until he arrives at the office, at which time new stimulation will occupy his attention and a new program will be selected to deal with it. If there were a mismatch when any feedback loop was completed, it would indicate that he had gone astray. Then he would adjust his behavior to produce a match—for instance, he would steer back to the road if he strayed off it. Or in the case of a gross mismatch —for example, if he were lost—a new program would be selected in an attempt to restore predictability.

For many years the reflex arc has been offered as the basic unit for analyzing behavior. Now there is a growing realization that the reflex arc provides an incomplete account of behavior. As the basic unit of analysis, the feedback loop includes the reflex functions of the individual. In addition, it offers a more comprehensive unit of analysis to account for behavior, for the individual is viewed as adjusting his behavior to environmental feedback on an ongoing basis, and sensory stimulation is seen not only as an initiator of behavior but also as the basis for testing predictions.

Our limited ability to understand mental process may have caused us to focus on the forces that we can observe with relative ease: the stimulus and the response. This perspective leads us to view the stimulus as the cause of the response, but the mental activity between the stimulus and the response tends to be overlooked as a force directing behavior.

With the feedback loop as the basic unit of analysis, the relationship between stimulation, mental activity, and response is viewed as cyclical. To investigate a behavior problem the student of behavior may enter the cycle at any point he wishes without neglecting any of the forces that contribute to behavior. Stimulus and response are seen as coexistent correlates. Observations of stimuli are used to guide responses toward a match between the prevailing program and ensuing events.

The matching process is continuous in that the individual is always attempting to maintain a predictable relationship with the environment by matching neuroprints with events. The matching process itself can be broken down into a continuing sequence of matchings as the individual attempts to make predictions.

The diagram in Figure 1 is a gross representation of the feedback loop and the sequence of matchings that are involved as the individual attempts to maintain a predictable relationship with his environment. As the diagram shows, the matching process breaks down into two component matching acts: matching for identification and matching for prediction. These acts may be described as follows.

Before predictions can be made about an event, the event must be to some extent familiar to the individual. Thus, the first stage of the matching process is matching for identification. When an existing event is matched with a neuroprint in the mind, the event may be identified as familiar. The matching makes it pos-

The Dynamics of Behavior

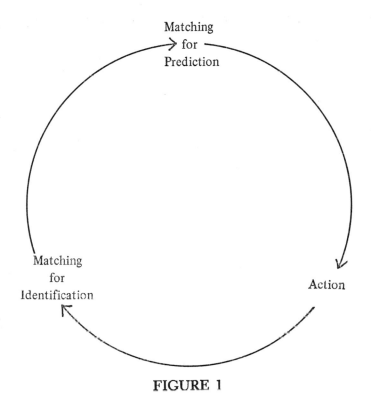

FIGURE 1

sible for the event to be predicted. On the other hand, when a match between an event and a neuroprint is not achieved, it indicates that the event may be totally unfamiliar and that no predictions can be made about it. Thus, identification is prerequisite to prediction.

If the event is totally unfamiliar, exposure to the event enables a neuroprint to form in the mind to represent that event. After the neuroprint is formed, the individual will subsequently be able to identify the event when it reappears, because a match can be obtained between the event and its corresponding neuroprint.

Once an event is matched with a neuroprint that generates arousal, a second matching ensues. The second matching is an attempt to predict ways of reducing the arousal. Such predictions can be obtained if a match is achieved between the simple neuroprint representing the arousing event and a more complex neuroprint, of which the simple neuroprint is a part, that portrays a sequence of events leading to the reduction of the arousal.

In other words, predictions are generated because simple neuroprints representing existing events that induce arousal form part of more complex neuroprints that portray transitions from existing states to future states that will result in the reduction of the arousal. When a simple neuroprint inducing arousal is elicited, causing the individual to identify an existing event, the simple neuroprint may in turn elicit a more complex neuroprint, of which it is a part, that portrays events that will lead to the reduction of the arousal. This will permit the individual to predict that the achievement of the events depicted by the complex neuroprint will lead to the reduction of the arousal. For the sake of convenience in future discussions, I shall call the complex neuroprint that describes a transition from a state of arousal to a future state in which the arousal is reduced a *master neuroprint*.

A master neuroprint, then, may be defined as a neuroprint that includes component neuroprints, representing an initiating event and the arousal associated with the event, a goal or future state predicted to reduce the arousal, and a program that prescribes a set of operations predicted to lead from the existing state to the goal.

These neuroprints will be symbolized as follows: A shall signify the component neuroprint that represents an initiating event that induces arousal; G shall signify the component neuroprint that represents a goal, the achievement of which is predicted to reduce the arousal; and P shall stand for the component neuroprint that represents a program that leads from the initiating event to the goal. Because most programs contain subroutines that represent a sequence of activities which lead to a goal, $P_1 \rightarrow P_2 \rightarrow P_3$, and so forth, will be used to represent a program and its various subroutines. The master neuroprint that is composed of these components shall be symbolized $A \rightarrow P \rightarrow G$. Thus, a master neuroprint shall portray a mental representation of a transition, by

THE DYNAMICS OF BEHAVIOR

means of a program, from an initiating event that induces arousal to a goal that reduces arousal. The program shall be subdivided into as many subroutines as needed to represent the various activities that are performed to achieve the goal.

It should be noted that the master neuroprint includes two predictions: the prediction of a future state or goal that will reduce arousal and the prediction that a particular program will lead to this goal. Although the two predictions are expressions of the same neuroprint, the goal represents a valued future state that the individual wants to achieve.

It is common for individuals to know what they want without knowing how to obtain it. Typically, there will be in the individual's mind more neuroprints that represent the goals he may wish to achieve than neuroprints that represent programs for achieving the goals.[5]

Matching for identification and prediction is governed by information-processing programs. However, when a match is made that generates the prediction of a goal that will reduce arousal and a motor program that will lead to the goal, the motor program portion of the master neuroprint will govern the individual's activities in pursuit of the goal.

After a program begins to govern the individual's actions, events are observed for identification once again to determine whether they are occurring as predicted. If events continue to occur as predicted, arousal will be reduced and the individual's attention can eventually turn to other matters.

The complete cycle of the matching process is illustrated in Figure 2. To understand the illustration, we need to assume that a master neuroprint portraying a transition from an arousing event to a goal that results in the reduction of the arousal may be elicited in the individual's mind. The master neuroprint may be expressed as follows: $A \rightarrow P_1 \rightarrow P_2 \rightarrow G$. Four events are portrayed by the master neuroprint. A represents the neuroprint of the initiating event and the arousal associated with it. $P_1 \rightarrow P_2$

---

[5] In Freudian parlance, the goal represents the object or event that is *cathected*. In the language of Kurt Lewin, the goal represents the object or event that has *valence* for the individual.

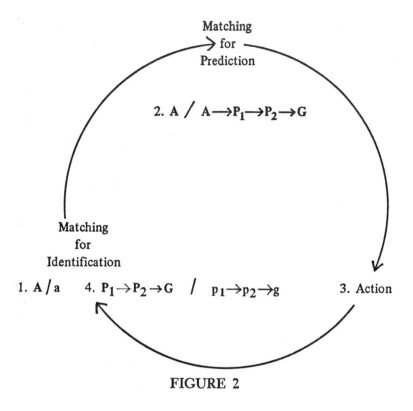

FIGURE 2

represents a neuroprint of a program that directs behavior from the arousing event to the goal, P_1 representing the first event to which the first subroutine of the program is predicted to lead on the way to the goal, and P_2 representing the second event to which the second subroutine of the program is expected to lead. G represents the event or goal that is predicted to result in the reduction of the arousal.

We can now trace the matching process from the initial matching for identification to matching for prediction and back to matching for identification in order to test the prediction.

Since **a** represents an event that occurs and is matched for identification, A / **a** at the bottom of the diagram, on the left, represents a match that is obtained between the event and a corresponding neuroprint in the mind. Assuming that a match for identification occurs and sufficient arousal is generated, the event will be identified and matching for prediction will begin. The neuroprint A will be matched with other neuroprints in the mind in search of a way to reduce the arousal. This will result in the match $A / A \to P_1 \to P_2 \to G$, if a match for prediction is achieved. The neuropoint A of the arousing event is matched with the master neuroprint $A \to P_1 \to P_2 \to G$ of which it is a part, because there is correspondence between them and the master neuroprint prescribes a goal that can be predicted to reduce the arousal and a program that can be predicted to lead from the arousing event to the goal. Once a master neuroprint has been selected, the program portions of it—$P_1 \to P_2$—proceed to direct behavior.

As the individual proceeds to act in accordance with the program, feedback is sought to test the predictions prescribed by the program. This involves matching for identification to determine whether the events through which the program is predicted to lead on the way to the goal are occurring as predicted. This match for identification can be expressed as follows: $P_1 \to P_2 \to G / p_1 \to p_2 \to g$. The program and goal portion—$P_1 \to P_2 \to G$ —of the master neuroprint predicts that behavior will be directed through events p_1 and p_2 and that the goal will be achieved as a result. Thus, the individual attempts to gain a more precise match by adjusting his actions to conform more closely to the program, or by adjusting the program. If, during the process, another event emerges that generates higher arousal than the prevailing event, it may supersede the prevailing event in dominating mental activity.

Let us consider an example in order to clarify the matching process.

Let us suppose that flies have landed on the individual in the past and he has learned to rid himself of the flies and the accompanying annoyance by fanning them away with his hand. The master neuroprint—$A \to P_1 \to P_2 \to G$—that may have formed as a result of the experience might be described as follows: A represents the experience of the fly landing on the individual and generating annoyance. $P_1 \rightarrow P_2$ represents the program directing the fanning action, P_1 perhaps representing the forward movement of the individual's hand, while P_2 represents the backward movement of his hand. G, the goal, represents the removal of the fly and the consequent reduction of the arousal.

Now let us suppose that a fly has just now landed on the individual. This event may be portrayed as a. A match for identification ensues. a will be matched with neuroprint A, because there is a closer correspondence of a to A than to other neuroprints stored in the mind. The match A / a will generate sufficient arousal for the fly to be identified as the annoying object, and a matching for prediction will commence.

The neuroprint A, portraying the annoying fly on the individual, will be matched with other neuroprints in the mind in search of a neuroprint that predicts the reduction of the arousal. This may result in the following match: $A / A \rightarrow P_1 \rightarrow P_2 \rightarrow G$. The neuroprint A, representing the annoying fly on the individual, is matched with the master neuroprint $A \rightarrow P_1 \rightarrow P_2 \rightarrow G$ of which it is a part, because the master neuroprint prescribes a goal that is predicted to result in the removal of the fly and the consequent reduction of arousal, as well as a program that prescribes behavior that will result in achieving the goal—fanning away the fly.

Once the master neuroprint has been selected, the program portion of it—$P_1 \rightarrow P_2$—controlling the fanning away of the fly, proceeds to direct behavior.

As he begins the fanning action, the individual attempts to determine whether the actions prescribed by the program are proceeding as predicted and whether the goal is being achieved. This requires him to seek a match between the actions involved in the fanning procedure that should result in the achievement of the goal and the neuroprint portraying these events—that is, $P_1 \rightarrow P_2 \rightarrow G / p_1 \rightarrow p_2 \rightarrow g$. Thus, as the individual proceeds with the fanning action, he is at least peripherally aware of whether his hand is moving backward and forward as the fanning program prescribes, and whether the execution of the program results in the removal of the fly and the reduction of the arousal.

He will strive to make his actions conform to the dictates of the program in an effort to remove the fly.

However, if the fly keeps on landing on him, he may change programs to remove the fly. For example, he may seek a fly swatter.

On the other hand, if another event occurs that induces higher arousal than the fly, his attention may be drawn to the other event and it may then dominate his mental activity. For example, if, during the fanning procedure, the individual should hit his hand on a hard object, thereby suffering considerable pain, his attention may be drawn away from the fly to his hurt hand until the pain subsides.

The above example illustrates a situation in which there is too little predictability. In this instance arousal has increased when a fly intruded. The individual seeks a match that will enable him to remove the fly. The same matching process applies to situations in which there is too much predictability—that is, during a monotonously prolonged match between events and neuroprints. The individual will then be impelled to pursue sufficient novelty to permit him to escape boredom. He will seek a situation that will be challenging and will enable him to extend his scope of prediction. Some illustrations of circumstances in which challenges are deliberately sought include playing games such as bridge or chess, solving crossword puzzles, and engaging in research (which may lead to discovery and invention).

When a program prescribes actions that are predicted to lead to a goal, and the actions actually do lead to that goal, the individual has gained control over his environment. He has learned how to take action so as to control the events that will lead to the goal in the future. The confirmation of prediction, therefore, can lead to control.

When a match for identification is achieved, the individual may be aware of what is happening and how he feels about it. (He may be aware that there is a fly on him and that it is annoying him.) When a match for prediction is achieved, the individual may be aware of what may happen and how he may feel about it. (He may be aware that the removal of the fly will relieve the annoyance.) Moreover, he may be aware of how the goal may be achieved. (He may be aware that by fanning his hand back and forth he may remove the fly from himself and relieve the annoyance.) After the program is employed to guide his behavior, he must test the predictions; he will attempt to ascertain whether events are happening as predicted and how he feels about the outcome. (He will attempt to determine whether the fanning action is being performed as the program prescribes and whether the execution of the program is resulting in the removal of the fly and the reduction of arousal.)

The individual has predicted the reduction of arousal introduced by an environmental intrusion through matching for identification and prediction. By acting in accordance with the master neuroprint selected, he was able to control events to reduce the arousal.

Thought is defined as the matching for identification and prediction that occurs in pursuit of correspondence between events and neuroprints in the mind. When a match exists between a neuroprint and a prevailing event the individual has achieved a predictable relationship with the environment. It is the purpose of thought to maintain predictability. Thought serves both to prepare for action and to guide action. It is involved in the preparation for action when an event intrudes and matching for identification and prediction ensue. It is involved in the guidance of action when a program has been selected to guide action and a match is sought between ensuing events and the program.

Various modes of thought will be discussed in chapters 9, 10, and 11. However, before we can continue with the discussion of thought we need to consider further the contribution of memory and abstraction to prediction and to describe neuroprint hierarchies.

6

Memories and Prediction

Memories permit predictions to be made about familiar events. When predictions are based on memories, the individual is prompted to predict that events will turn out in the future as they have in the past, because memories are mental representations of past experiences. Thus, when an impinging event elicits a memory, the future outcome portrayed by the memory to which the event leads will have been experienced before.

The example used in the previous chapter, of an individual fanning an annoying fly off himself, is a case in point. The master neuroprint that directed the individual's behavior was a memory. The memory was formed from previous experience in which he successfully removed flies by fanning them with his hand. So, when a fly lands on him, he can predict that the fanning action will remove the fly in the present in the same way that it has done in the past.

This example and the diagram shown in the previous chapter provide a comprehensive picture of the way in which memories generate identification and prediction. Now we shall consider some differences between identification and prediction.

Basically, identification may require an understanding of space relationships only, whereas prediction requires an understanding of both space and time relationships. An event can be recognized by its composition and in contrast to its background. However, in order for an event to be predicted, the individual must understand what the event may become in the future. Let me illustrate the difference.

Suppose that a person's repeated exposure to the geometric form of an angle results in the formation of the memory of an angle in his mind. The actual angle and the memory may be symbolized as shown in Figure 3. When the angle subsequently

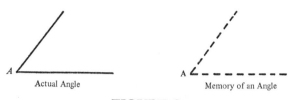

Actual Angle   Memory of an Angle

FIGURE 3

appears, it will be matched with the various neuroprints in the mind, and because it matches more closely the memory of an angle than other neuroprints, the memory of the angle will be elicited and (assuming sufficient arousal or interest) the object will be identified as an angle. The identification of the angle requires only an understanding of spatial relationships—that is, an understanding of the composition of an angle in contrast to its background at a single point in time.

Suppose that the recognition of a triangle is learned in the same way as that of an angle. The triangle and its corresponding memory may be symbolized as shown in Figure 4. In order to recognize the triangle, the individual will need to understand the composition of the triangle in contrast to its background. This means that the individual must understand the relationships between the

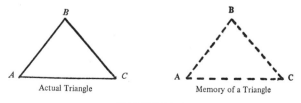

Actual Triangle   Memory of a Triangle

FIGURE 4

parts of a triangle and the whole, or he must know that a triangle is a closed figure composed of three angles. However, this understanding is not sufficient to permit him to make predictions about the triangle. To make such predictions, he will need to have an understanding of the temporal characteristics that are related to the composition of the triangle. For example, he will need to understand a triangle well enough to draw one, because the drawing of a triangle requires the ability to arrange the composition of the parts in time.

Once the individual understands the temporal as well as the spatial relationships involved in the construction of triangles, it is possible that exposure to a part of a triangle may bring the whole triangle to his mind. As Donald O. Hebb indicates, in the early stages of perceptual development, the mental representation of the whole triangle might be elicited only after repeated activation of **A, B, C,** but later it might be brought to mind following sensory activation of **A** alone, so that the triangle would be recognized with a single glance at A.[1]

This might be represented as shown in Figure 5.

FIGURE 5

In order to clarify time and space relationships, let me apply the matching process described in the previous chapter to the following example involving construction of a triangle. Suppose an individual who knows how to draw a triangle is observing a friend drawing a triangle. The drawing of the triangle is posited to introduce the dimension of time. As the angles of the triangle are being drawn, they are matched with memories of similar figures

[1] *The Organization of Behavior*, p. 100.

for identification. If a match is achieved and sufficient arousal is induced, the angles will be identified.

The memory of the angles being drawn are then matched with the master neuroprints in the mind for prediction in order to determine what the figure is becoming. As the drawing of the triangle progresses toward completion, a match will be achieved between the memory of the angles drawn and the master neuroprint displaying the transition to a triangle. This will occur because eventually there will be a closer match between the drawing of the angles and a master neuroprint memory predicting the construction of a triangle than between the drawing and memories predicting the construction of other geometric forms.

The arousing neuroprint contained in the memory forming a master neuroprint represents the angles that are being drawn at the time. The arousal initiated by the memory of the drawing represents the curiosity or interest the onlooker has in determining what the incomplete figure may become. The individual's desire to predict will prompt him to regard any transition as a challenge, and he will attempt to predict the outcome that should occur after the transition has been completed.

The program portions of the master neuroprint memory govern the operations the individual performs in observing his friend, and it depicts the sequence of events he expects to occur as his friend proceeds to draw.

The individual observes the progress of the drawing, and seeks a match between his memory of how a triangle is drawn to completion and the actual drawing of the geometric figure. During this process a matching for identification occurs and a testing of the predictions indicated in the master neuroprint memory takes place. It is important to note, concerning time relationships, that the program neuroprint charts the transition that takes place with time and the forces that control the transition.

It may seem that the appearance of a figure would not generate much arousal in an individual. However, if we are to give credence to the individual's desire to predict, we must realize that he is interested in making predictions about anything in transition. Moreover, the Gestalt psychologists suggest that individuals seek closure, and, according to that theory, the appearance of an incomplete figure would cause the individual to form it into a complete figure so as to realize closure. Wertheimer describes the Gestalt view of closure.[2]

The Gestalt concept of closure can be interpreted within the framework of the theory presented in this book. I agree that individuals seek closure. However, closure to me means two things. First, when an incomplete figure appears, the individual will attempt to complete it mentally. For example, a partial triangle may bring to mind the idea of a whole triangle. However, considering prediction as the basic motive, the act of completing mentally an incomplete figure represents the individual's prediction of what the incomplete figure might become in the future. Thus, mental closure represents an idea of a predicted outcome.

The second meaning of closure is concerned with the individual's desire to confirm his predictions. The individual not only seeks to predict, but once a prediction is made he seeks closure in the form of a confirmation of his prediction. In this sense, the individual seeks a match between a neuroprint in his mind generating a prediction and ensuing events, in an effort to confirm his predictions. When a prediction is confirmed, an issue may be said to be closed and the individual may be said to have achieved satisfaction. Thus, in one sense, closure is achieved when the individual has an idea of an outcome that he predicts may occur. In this second sense, closure is achieved when the prediction is confirmed.

Both identification and prediction involve an understanding of the relationship between parts and wholes. With respect to the understanding that is gained through recognition, the parts add up to the whole, and nothing more. The elements of an object to which the individual is exposed are recognized only as the elements that are present. With respect to the understanding that is involved in prediction, the whole is greater than the sum of its parts in the sense that the individual not only has an idea of what is the initiating event, but he also has an idea of outcomes that may be generated by the initiating event in the future.

In Gestalt psychology there is also an emphasis on the tendency to see wholes. If we regard the tendency to see wholes in terms

[2] Max Wertheimer, "Laws of Organization in Perceptual Forms," p. 83.

of the dynamic implications for prediction as well as in terms of static implications, that point of view fits into the framework of the theory I am presenting here. From this perspective, identification depends upon understanding the static spatial relationships that permit an event to be identified because of its distinct composition in contrast to its background; the whole here represents the figure in contrast to its background. Prediction depends upon an understanding of the dynamic spatial and temporal relationships of an event in transition; the whole in this case includes the event and what the event may turn out to be with the passage of time.

However, it seems, at the least, unreasonable, and perhaps even highly untenable, to maintain that individuals see static relationships at the expense of seeing dynamic relationships that change with time. It seems more accurate to contend that stable relationships enhance understanding, whether the relationships be static or dynamic. Even a dynamic relationship that is changing with time must change with some semblance of order to permit the relationship to be understood. This is how I prefer to interpret the meaning of the "good Gestalt." This point of view permits acceptance of the dynamics of change without denying the unity of the whole.

Referring to the law of Prägnanz in Gestalt psychology, Köhler has stated: "Every state of rest or stationary equilibrium which occurs in nature is *a unique case* in contrast with an infinite manifold of other states. . . . *In all processes ending in a state independent of time, development is in the direction of minimal energy in the ultimate structure.*"[3]

Lindmann spoke of the law of Prägnanz in the following terms: "This terminal form (of a vision) is governed by the law of Prägnanz: it must assume the best possible shape."[4] Wulf elaborates on this view. He states that "The most general law underlying all change is the Law of Prägnanz according to which every Gestalt becomes as 'good' as possible."[5]

[3] Wolfgang Köhler, "Physical Gestalten," pp. 51–52.
[4] E. Lindmann, "Gamma Movement," p. 181.
[5] Friedrich Wulf, "Tendencies in Figural Variation," p. 148.

Memories and Predictions

Gestalt principles seem to hold when the time element is introduced to show transition. In general, the law of Prägnanz can be said to assert that maximum stability in the preceptual field promotes both identification and prediction because the stable relationship of events in the field promotes the association of the events in the mind. The inclusion of time as a dimension of understanding simply suggests that prediction is enhanced when there is an orderly transition from an existing form to an emerging form so that the relationship between the two forms can be identified and predicted.

Finally, from the vantage point of the present theory, there is no contradiction between behaviorism theory and the field approach of Gestalt psychology. The Gestalt law of Prägnanz defines the field arrangements that support the formation of memories. Behaviorism theory defines how factors that govern the individual's exposure to an event determine whether a memory of the event will form. For example, the frequency, recency, and intensity of exposure to an event tend to determine whether a memory of the event will form and be maintained.

7

ABSTRACTIONS AND PREDICTION

Having considered the relationship between memories and prediction, we can proceed to a discussion of the relationship between abstractions and prediction, examining at this point a most basic and pertinent aspect of mental process: the transfer of knowledge.

One of the more popular explanations of transfer of knowledge or learning was offered by Edward L. Thorndike. A full statement of his position appeared as early as 1903 in his *Educational Psychology*. Thorndike contended that transfer depends on identical elements between old learning and the new learning that the old learning facilitates. Thus, when a new activity is learned more easily because of an activity that was learned previously, it is attributable to the overlap or common elements in the two activities. Thorndike's explanation of transfer grew out of the extensive research he conducted.[1]

The basic interpretation of transfer offered by Thorndike has been both explicitly and implicitly endorsed by many psychologists who have succeeded him. It remains for us to consider how transfer of knowledge is explained within the context of the theory presented here.

When a match for prediction has been achieved, transfer of knowledge takes place because neuroprints in the mind that represent stored information obtained from past experience are being

[1] Thorndike's theories are discussed in Ernest R. Hilgard, *Theories of Learning*, pp. 19–51.

applied to predict a current event. Thus, the only time that transfer cannot occur is when the individual is confronted with a totally unfamiliar situation, which he must then memorize.

However, transfer requires more than the identification and matching of elements that are common to an old and a new event. Events themselves may have identical elements, but it is not only the elements that two events may have in common that permit transfer to occur. The transfer occurs when, in the match for prediction, a neuroprint of a past experience finds a match with a master neuroprint. If the memory of a past experience has not been established, or if an established neuroprint is not matched with a master neuroprint when a match for prediction is sought, transfer will not take place, even though an old experience may share a great many identical elements with the new experience confronting the individual.

I have symbolized a match for prediction as $A / A \rightarrow P \rightarrow G$; when such a match has been achieved, transfer of knowledge has occurred. During the process of matching for prediction, transfer may be based either on memories or on abstractions.

We have seen how transfer based on memory may take place, as in the example concerning the fanning away of an annoying fly. In this example the components of the master neuroprint $A \rightarrow P \rightarrow G$ were as follows: A represented a memory of an annoying fly landing on the individual. The memory A was matched with the memory $A \rightarrow P_1 \rightarrow P_2 \rightarrow G$ of which it was a part, because the master neuroprint memory prescribed a goal predicted to result in the removal of the fly and the consequent reduction of arousal, as well as a program that prescribed behavior to achieve the goal. The master neuroprint memory was predicted to remove the fly and reduce arousal because the individual remembered that it had done so in the past.

When transfer is based on memory, the event to be predicted is familiar. The master neuroprint memory used to predict the event has usually been used before in similar situations, so its application is also familiar. When transfer is based on memory, it often involves the execution of a habit, such as the automatic fanning away of the fly in the above example; habits are used to

THE THEORY

predict familiar events. Moreover, when transfer is based on memory, it is implicit that the individual will deal with the new situation in the same way he dealt with similar situations in the past.

The relationship between abstractions and prediction also plays a significant part in the process of transfer.

An abstraction was defined as a category of memories that have been grouped together because they have similar characteristics. The assertion that individuals categorize their experiences is amply supported in the literature on the subject. In their book *A Study of Thinking*, Bruner, Goodnow, and Austin suggest that people tend to categorize events because categorization simplifies the environment for them; it reduces the need for learning, since new events are viewed as belonging to old categories, and it facilitates identification when objects can be recognized as members of categories.

For Piaget, the process of categorizing is an important aspect of mental development. The ability to classify experiences indicates when the child has reached the "concrete operations" stage of development. The operation of classifying is considered the mental equivalent to the motor act of grouping together objects recognized as similar. The ability to classify objects is illustrated in a study reported by Piaget and Szeminski entitled *The Child's Concept of Numbers*.

The *schema*—Piaget's term for the mental representation of events—is considered to be based upon common elements. Inhelder, Piaget's associate, defines a schema as "the structure common to all those acts which—from the subject's point of view—are equivalent."[2] It should also be noted that the Gestalt law of similarity (which states, in essence, that in perception individuals tend to group similar events together) reinforces the position that individuals tend to categorize their experiences.

Travers summarizes the process of categorizing as follows: "The processes of generalization and discrimination are seen to operate in categorizing behavior, an important aspect of behavior through

[2] Baerbal Inhelder and Jean Piaget, *The Growth of Logical Thinking*, p. 122.

ABSTRACTION AND PREDICTION

which the countless situations and events encountered by the learner are grouped. Both human and subhuman animals demonstrate through their behavior this tendency to categorize the situations they encounter."[3]

The products of the categorization of experiences have been well known since the early days of psychological research. Studies in stimulus and response generalization demonstrate the effects of categorization. For example, stimulus generalization was demonstrated in Pavlov's training of dogs. Dogs conditioned to raise a front paw each time a tone of 440 vibrations per second is sounded will make the same response when a tone of 220 vibrations per second is sounded. Response generalization has also been demonstrated in research when one stimulus is shown to elicit a range of responses in the individual.

With these implications for the process of abstraction, we can consider the relevance of abstraction in the context of the present theory.

Abstractions permit the individual to make predictions about the relatively unfamiliar, the novel, and the unknown through the transfer of knowledge. When predictions are based on memory, the individual will predict that events will turn out in the future as they have in the past. Abstractions permit predictions to be made about events that have not occurred before in the individual's experience.

For example, a baby may learn that his mother will bring a toy to him if he asks for it. This memory permits the baby to predict that if he asks, his mother will bring a toy to him. He may eventually learn the same thing about his sister and father, and be able to acquire toys from them in the same way. Once the baby learns that all people can bring him toys, the abstraction "people" might form on this common basis, and he would realize that anyone fitting the category would be able to bring toys to him. On a subsequent occasion, if he saw a stranger he would realize that although he had never seen that particular person before, the person could bring toys to him.

The matching process might proceed as follows. The stranger

[3] Robert M. W. Travers, *Essentials of Learning*, p. 143.

who appears does not correspond to any of the baby's memories, so the baby does not recognize him as familiar. However, certain features of the stranger are recognized as familiar, and the memory of these features are matched with abstractions in an attempt to make some prediction about him. The memory of the familiar features of the stranger match the features that are common to the abstraction "people" (if the abstraction has been formed), and the baby identifies the stranger as a person. Subsequently, when a match for prediction is achieved, the baby realizes that he can make the same general predictions about the stranger that he can make about other people. He might then ask the stranger for a toy. In this way abstractions are used to transfer knowledge to an unfamiliar situation.

It must be emphasized that identification is prerequisite to prediction and that a totally unfamiliar event cannot be identified at the time it first appears. To identify a totally unfamiliar event, the individual must be exposed to it over a period of time until a neuroprint that represents the event has formed in his mind.

The example cited above can be applied to the model of the matching process as follows:

MATCHING FOR IDENTIFICATION: A / a. The stranger is matched with memories in the mind, and no match is achieved. The features of the stranger are then matched with abstractions in search of identification. (The matching of an event with a memory is attempted first, because a closer or more detailed fit can be obtained between an event and a memory than between an event and an abstraction, and a more detailed fit between a neuroprint and an event promotes the precision of prediction.) When the features of the stranger (a) are matched with the abstraction "people" (A), the stranger is identified as a person.

MATCHING FOR PREDICTION: $A / A \rightarrow P \rightarrow G$. The neuroprint of the abstraction "people" is then matched with other neuroprints in the mind in search of a prediction. Consequently, a match is achieved between the neuroprint "people" (A) and a master neuroprint that portrays people bringing toys to him on request $(A \rightarrow P \rightarrow G)$. In the master neuroprint, A represents the abstraction "people." G represents the goal that is predicted to result in the acquisition of toys, and **P** represents the program that portrays the actions that are predicted to lead to the acquisition of toys. The program will portray the actions of the baby in asking for a toy and the actions the stranger is expected to take to deliver the toy.

ACTION: **P**. Once a match for prediction is achieved, the program leading to the acquisition of toys will be implemented—that is, the baby will ask the stranger for a toy.

MATCHING FOR IDENTIFICATION (testing the prediction): $P \rightarrow G$ / $p \rightarrow g$. As the execution of the program proceeds, the baby seeks a match between the neuroprint portraying the programmed events leading to the goal ($P \rightarrow G$) and the actual events that occur ($p \rightarrow g$), in anticipation of the acquisition of a toy. If the stranger is not prompt in responding to the baby's request, the baby may modify his behavior to gain confirmation of his prediction. He may repeat his request in more beseeching tones. With continued thwarting, another program may be selected to acquire the toy: the baby may begin to cry.

In this illustration we have seen how abstractions permit transfer so that unfamiliar events may be predicted. Memories of objects are categorized on the basis of their common characteristics to form abstractions. When a somewhat novel stimulus has characteristics that match the characteristics of an abstraction, unfamiliar events can be predicted by matching the familiar elements of an unfamiliar stimulus with the elements of an abstraction. The prediction of novel events through abstraction is what psychologists usually refer to as insight.

Insight is often characterized as an experience in which the individual suddenly understands a relationship he did not understand before. Insight serves to refer to the moment in the transfer process that a match is achieved between a novel sensory event and an abstraction that enables the individual to understand and predict the sensory event. In reference to the example cited, insight would refer to the moment the baby matched the characteristics of the stranger with the abstraction "people" and was able to predict that the stranger could bring toys to him.

Insight, then, is a form of discovery, and abstractions provide the basis for discovery. When an unfamiliar event is matched with an abstraction, the individual has discovered something about the event. When he confirms the predictions generated by the abstraction, he has confirmed the discovery. For example, when the baby matches the features of the stranger with the abstraction "people," and then a match for prediction is achieved indicating that people can deliver toys, insight has occurred; the baby has discovered that the stranger can bring toys to him. When he asks the stranger for a toy and the stranger brings it, the discovery has been confirmed. Now, any individual's insight is a discovery, even though his personal discovery may be common knowledge. The difference between a personal discovery and an invention is that in invention the product of the insight is new to all men.

An important aspect of transfer is that it can occur without immediate sensory support. Transfer occurs when a match for prediction is achieved, and a match for prediction may be achieved either when the individual is confronted by an event or afterward. In the above example, the baby may realize that the stranger may bring toys to him while the stranger is in his presence or after the stranger has gone. In the latter case, the identification of the stranger with the abstraction "people" lingers after the stranger has gone. Subsequently, a match for prediction may occur that indicates that the stranger is able to bring toys. The mind can function in this way, free of sensory stimulation, to make predictions. Thus, the individual is not "stimulus-bound." Some stimulus-response theorists exaggerate the influence of sensory stimulation in directing responses. Memories can interact with other memories and abstractions to direct responses.

In the matching process, identification is initiated by sensory stimulation, because it is the matching of the initiating event with memories or abstractions that induces identification. On the other hand, prediction is not induced by the initiating event but, rather, by a matching of a memory or an abstraction of an event with a master neuroprint that includes a portrayal of the outcomes to which the event may lead in the future. Thus, the matching that yields prediction occurs strictly within the mind.

Furthermore, matching for prediction will not proceed unless the memory of the initiating event induces sufficient arousal when matching for identification occurs. If high arousal is induced, prediction may be pursued after the initiating event has ceased to stimulate the individual, because it is the memory or abstraction of an event that induces arousal, not the event itself. In fact, prediction may be sought for as long as the memory or abstraction of the initiating event continues to induce sufficiently high arousal. If the memory or abstraction of the initiating event in question is superseded by a second memory or abstraction that generates higher arousal, the memory or abstraction of the initiating event may return to induce the pursuit of prediction again, after the second memory or abstraction no longer prevails. Mental process may thus proceed without being controlled by immediate events, for it is the memory or abstraction of events, not the presence of the events, that induces mental activity.

Ideas can be brought to mind in one of four ways:

1. A stimulus can bring an idea to mind by eliciting a memory or an abstraction associated with it.

2. An instinct can bring an idea to mind by eliciting a memory or an abstraction associated with it.

3. A memory can bring an idea to mind by eliciting another memory or an abstraction associated with it.

4. An abstraction can bring an idea to mind by eliciting a memory or another abstraction associated with it.

Memories and abstractions not only induce ideas themselves; they also elicit other memories and abstractions that induce other ideas.

Abstractions permit the individual to make choices, because the memories in a category or an abstraction have something in common. Abstractions generate ideas about the similarities and differences among events. The memories in a category may provide alternative goals that may lead to the reduction of arousal and alternative programs for pursuing the same goal. This makes it possible for the individual to choose from among various goals and programs.

For instance, the abstraction "food" includes items that have in common the fact that they may be eaten to reduce hunger.

THE THEORY

For any individual, the abstraction "food" will include all of the items that he knows can be eaten. When he is hungry, he may choose from among the various food products an item he desires or values and seek to acquire it as a goal. If the item cannot be acquired, he may choose another item in the category.

Programs may also form abstractions. The programs that lead to the acquisition of milk as a goal, for example, may be categorized together to form an abstraction. This abstraction may include programs that prescribe different ways of obtaining milk. One program might lead to the refrigerator in one's home, while another program might lead to a restaurant. The exercise of choice will be discussed in chapter 9, where deliberation is considered.

In this chapter, I have attempted to explain how transfer of knowledge occurs through memories and abstractions and to interpret the use of abstractions in prediction and thought. The motive to predict induces the comparison of stimuli and neuroprints for similarities and differences, and consequently generates the formation of abstractions. The comparison for similarities and differences is the basis for matching and prediction. The resulting formation of abstractions improves prediction because it permits relatively unfamiliar events to be predicted.

Abstractions provide the basis for gaining insight and making choices and, in general, permit the individual to combine and recombine his memories in a myriad of ways. A given event or program may be associated with many different abstractions, enabling a given program or event to be used in many different ways. Insight gained through abstractions allows events and programs to be used in new ways that lead to discovery and invention.

8

THE ORGANIZATION OF
NEUROPRINT HIERARCHIES

In chapter 4, I described the development of neuroprints. In this chapter, I shall describe the way in which neuroprints develop into hierarchies and are stored, retrieved, and applied to facilitate prediction. There are a number of different types of hierarchical organizations. It is my belief that neuroprints are organized into what is generally referred to as representational hierarchies. A representational hierarchy is a hierarchy in which the lower levels are represented in higher levels and development at the lower levels is often prerequisite to development at the higher levels.

At the lowest level of the neuroprint hierarchy are reflexes, the inherited neuroprints that govern behavior in an automatic, inflexible, and involuntary manner (e.g., the sucking response). Reflexes are the first neuroprints stored in the mind.

Tropisms—instincts that can operate with some degree of flexibility—represent the second level of the neuroprint hierarchy. Examples of tropisms cited earlier were the nest-building instincts of birds and the sex instinct.

Habits form the third level of the hierarchy. Habits are learned neuroprints, or memories. Like reflexes, they also govern behavior automatically, inflexibly, and involuntarily. Primitive habits tend to be extensions of reflexes. Reflexes seem to be prerequisite to the formation of habits and are represented in habits. For example, the habit of drinking from a baby bottle may be an extension of the sucking response. The ability to suck appears to be prerequisite to the ability to drink from a baby bottle, and sucking is represented in the process.

Flexible programs constitute the fourth level of the hierarchy. A flexible program is a memory that defines a set of behaviors that can be performed in more than one order. For example, the order in which one drinks the fruit juice and water placed on the dinner table is optional. Habits may be represented in flexible programs; for instance, the habit of drinking from a glass is represented in the flexible program described above. Of course, programs may provide various degrees of flexibility with respect to the behaviors they prescribe.

Abstractions, which are categories of similar memories, make up the fifth level of the hierarchy. The formation of abstractions permits insight and a choice of behavior. The possibility of making a choice from among alternative behaviors lends considerable flexibility to behavior. For example, when the abstraction "beverage" forms, the individual may be aware that he can drink any item in the category to quench his thirst.

Additional levels of the neuroprint hierarchy form as similar lower-level abstractions are grouped together to form higher-level abstractions. For instance, the abstractions "beverage" and "food" may be grouped together to form the higher-level abstraction "nutrients." The highest possible level of abstraction might be thought of as "the individual in his environment." This abstraction would include all the neuroprints that related the individual to his environment and therefore permit him to make predictions about the relationship.

Some of the work of Newell, Simon, and Shaw suggests that the mind may store information in representational hierarchies. Their work was primarily concerned with computer simulation of logical processes.[1]

The impressive work of Robert T. Gagné has contributed a great deal to the extension of traditional learning theory. Gagné describes learning as developing within the framework of a representational hierarchy. He not only contends that early learning is

[1] Allen Newell and Herbert A. Simon, "The Logic Machine"; Allen Newell and John C. Shaw, "Programming the Logic Theory Machine."

represented in later learning but he shows, in addition, that within the hierarchy certain learning at lower levels is prerequisite to learning at higher levels. Gagné states that "The subjects of school instruction possess hierarchical organizations with respect to the required types of learning. Each can be analysed to reveal prerequisite learnings that grow progressively simple as one works downward from principles to $S \rightarrow R$ connections. The learning of principles that are usually the most obvious objectives of instruction requires the previous learning of other principles, and these in turn require prerequisite concepts, multiple discrimination, verbal sequences, and $S \rightarrow R$ connections."[2] Gagné diagrams the hierarchical capabilities learned during instruction in reading (pp. 200–1).

Although Gagné's hierarchical structure is tailored primarily to indicate instructional sequences, it does point out that learning proceeds according to representational hierarchies from the simple to the complex, and that simpler learnings are prerequisite to and represented in the more complex learnings in the hierarchies. Gagné's specific description of learning hierarchies appears to fit within the general definition of a neuroprint hierarchy offered at the beginning of this chapter. What Gagné refers to as $S \rightarrow R$ learning, chaining, and verbal sequences would come under the heading of habits. Verbal sequences might include some flexibility with respect to their ordering. Multiple discriminations concepts and principles refer to abstractions at a progressively higher level.

The neuroprints stored in the hierarchical fashion described above are ready to be retrieved for prediction in the following manner:

The correspondence between an event and a neuroprint is the basis on which an event elicits a neuroprint when a match for identification is sought. Similarly, when a match for prediction is sought, the degree of correspondence between two neuroprints determines whether a match will occur. In the matching process, the closer the correspondence between an event and a neuroprint, or between two neuroprints, the greater the probability that a match will occur.

[2] Robert T. Gagné, *The Conditions of Learning*, p. 202.

For example, a greater correspondence can be achieved between an event and a memory than between an event and an abstraction, because a memory, being a neuroprint of a specific experience, represents the experience in detail, whereas an abstraction is a general representation of the similarities within a category of memories, not a specific representation of any one of the events in the category. It is as if a memory were a key made to fit a specific lock in every detail, while an abstraction is a master key which fits a number of similar locks, because it has one cut that is common to all of them but which fits none of the locks in particular.

This suggests that if a match for identification can be achieved at a lower level of the neuroprint hierarchy, it will be achieved there. For instance, if an event corresponds to both a memory and an abstraction, the memory will probably be elicited because there can be greater correspondence between an event and a memory than between an event and an abstraction. If a match is achieved between an event and an abstraction, rather than between an event and a memory, it may be because a memory of the event has not formed as yet—that is, the individual probably has not had sufficient encounters with the event for a memory to have become established.

The nature of the retrieval process seems to promote adaptation, because a match for identification obtained at a lower level of the neuroprint hierarchy will probably lead to a more accurate prediction than will a match achieved at a higher level. Let me clarify this point.

First, the event is matched with a neuroprint at some level of the neuroprint hierarchy in order for the event to be identified. If the event is matched at a lower level of the neuroprint hierarchy, it will be identified in greater detail for the reasons already given.

Second, during matching for prediction, the neuroprint representing the event is matched with a master neuroprint. If the neuroprint representing the event is on a lower level of the neuroprint hierarchy, it will be defined in greater detail; it therefore has the potential of fitting a master neuroprint in greater detail. For example, a memory defines an event in greater detail than does an abstraction, and consequently, when a memory represents an event, it has the potential of matching a master neuroprint in greater detail when a match for prediction is attempted.

When a match for prediction is achieved in greater detail, there is a greater potential for predictive accuracy because when there is greater correspondence, the prediction can be, in a sense, more specifically tailored for the event. For instance, an item can be matched for identification with a memory of an apple only if an apple has been seen before. When the memory of the apple is matched for prediction with a master neuroprint and as a result the apple is eaten, it is because apples have been safely eaten before and have satisfied the individual's hunger in the past. The prediction generated by the master neuroprint indicating that the apple will satisfy his hunger, without producing adverse side effects, most probably will prove to be accurate.

On the other hand, when an unfamiliar object is matched for identification with the abstraction "food," that abstraction is matched for prediction with the master neuroprint that governs the eating process. When the match is achieved and action is taken, there is less probability that the object will satisfy the individual's hunger and a greater possibility that he may poison himself.

In matching for prediction, then, the greater the correspondence between the neuroprint of an event and the master neuroprint elicited to predict the event, the more probable it will be that the event will be predicted precisely. Further, in the match for prediction, there will be a greater potential for detailed correspondence of the neuroprint representing the event with a master neuroprint if a match for identification has been achieved at a lower level of the neuroprint hierarchy.

It should be understood that I am describing a natural tendency that contributes to the accuracy of prediction. However, the degree of correspondence between an event and a neuroprint or between two neuroprints is only one factor that contributes to the accuracy of prediction. More will be said about the accuracy of prediction in the next chapter.

Because of the individual's desire to predict, neuroprints tend to be stored in such a way that arousing events are related to goals that can be predicted to reduce the arousal and to programs that lead from the initiating events to the goals. I have called such a composition of simple neuroprints a master neuroprint because it includes the elements necessary to generate the predictions needed to reduce arousal.

When a neuroprint representing an arousing event matches a master neuroprint, the goal predicted to reduce arousal is selected and the program predicted to lead to the goal is selected also. However, a match can be made that prescribes the desired goal but not the program that leads to it. People are often aware of what they want without knowing how to obtain it. The point is, nevertheless, that simple neuroprints appear to be organized into master neuroprints so that events inducing arousal, goals predicted to reduce the arousal, and programs leading to the goals are related to one another if existing information stored in the mind permits them to be related in this way.

If this is the case, master neuroprints will be organized within the hierarchical structure of neuroprints so that when a match for identification is achieved within the hierarchy and arousal is generated, the subsequent matching for prediction can readily elicit the means of reducing the arousal.

Programs function as parts of neuroprint hierarchies. However, it is important to note that programs are themselves organized in a hierarchical manner.

A program may be very simple in that it may contain one operation for which only one prediction is made, or it may be very complex in that it may include a series of operations that lead through a series of predictions culminating in the prediction of a particular outcome. A complex program is organized as a hierarchy of simple programs. The simple programs I have called subroutines of the more complex programs, as they are entitled in the language of computer programming.

Perhaps the best presentation of program hierarchies is offered by Miller, Galanter, and Pribram[3] in their analysis of what they

[3] George A. Miller, Eugene Galanter, and Karl H. Pribram, *Plans and the Structure of Behavior*, p. 34.

call TOTE. TOTE is a description of the elements of the feedback loop, which are specified as Test-Operate-Test-Exit. The initial test phase involves a test of the congruity between the selected programs and sensory stimulations. If there is incongruity, operations proceed in accordance with the program to gain congruity. Then another test for congruity is made. The operation is repeated until a test reveals that there is congruity, at which time the program is completed.

In a simple program for hammering a nail, the nail is tested for congruity in the first test phase to determine whether the head is sticking up. If it is, the operation of hammering is started. Then the next test is made. If the head is still sticking up, the hammering is repeated until the head is flush, at which time the program is completed and control of behavior by the program will stop (exit).

A complex program breaks down into a number of subroutines that are organized in a hierarchical manner. To continue with the example of hammering, the hammering program consists of subroutines, one subroutine for lifting the hammer and one for striking the nail.

The program is described by Miller, Galanter, and Pribram in the following manner: "We should expect the sequence of events to run off in this order: Test nail. (Head sticks up.) Test hammer. (Hammer is down.) Lift hammer. Test hammer. (Hammer is up.) Test hammer. (Hammer is up.) Strike nail. Test hammer. (Hammer is down.) Test nail. (Head sticks up.) Test hammer. And so on, until the test of the nail reveals that its head is flush with the surface of the work, at which point control can be transferred elsewhere. Thus the compound of TOTE *units unravels itself simply enough into a coordinated sequence of tests and actions, although the underlying structure that organizes and coordinates the behavior is itself hierarchical, not sequential. . . .* Note that it is the *operational* phase of the TOTE that is expanded into a list of other TOTE units."

Upon completion, each subroutine is tested through a feedback loop in the order prescribed by the program. When a feedback loop indicates a match between a subroutine and sensory feedback, the prediction of that subroutine has been fulfilled. Then the next subroutine can be executed and tested via a feedback loop in the same manner. The subroutines are executed and tested in succession until the larger feedback loop defined by the total program has been completed as predicted.

During each of the subroutines the actions of the individual are adjusted to gain a match between sensory feedback and the prevailing program; if a gross mismatch occurs, a new program must be selected to guide action. In the hammering program, if the nail is being driven into the board crookedly, subsequent strokes with the hammer will be adjusted to straighten the nail. On the other hand, if the nail is too crooked to be straightened as it is being driven into the board, it will be necessary to use the claw end of the hammer to straighten the nail—in which case a new program controlling the use of the claw must be selected to straighten the nail. Then the initial hammering program can be reinstated to finish the job.

From this example, it can be seen that programs are related and that if one program, such as the hammering program, does not generate congruity, another program may be elicited, such as the program directing the operations of the claw end of the hammer, to assist in achieving the goal. Thus, the feedback from the testing of one program provides the occasion upon which another program may be elicited.

Programs develop into hierarchies progressing from instincts to habits to more flexible programs as the individual matures. The more automatic programs that have been inherited as reflexes or learned earlier in life as habits are not only represented in the formation of the more sophisticated programs learned later but are also included as subroutines of those programs.

In the neuroprint hierarchy of levels of representation, higher levels of the hierarchy are an extension of the lower levels and to an extent represent them, and may therefore be substituted for the lower levels in the pursuit of a match for identification and prediction. There seems to be a remarkable adaptive logic that lies behind the organization of neuroprint hierarchies, if these conjectures are correct. The accuracy of prediction is promoted

The Organization of Neuroprint Hierarchies

because a match is obtained on the basis of the "tightness of fit" between an event and a neuroprint, or between two neuroprints, in pursuit of a prediction. This results in a match being obtained on a lower level of the hierarchy, a result which produces a match that is more representative of the event to be predicted. And the more representative of an event a neuroprint is, the greater the probability that the prediction generated will be accurate. Furthermore, when a match cannot be achieved at a lower level, it is still possible to obtain a prediction through a match at a higher level, for the lower levels of the hierarchy are represented in the higher levels. Thus, the hierarchical arrangement promotes the selection of the "best" possible prediction from among alternatives.

The hierarchical organization of programs also seems to be extraordinarily adaptive in that the reflexes present at birth become incorporated into habits when habits are learned. These habits are incorporated into the more flexible programs that are learned later in life. In this way simple programs may be incorporated into more complex programs as the individual matures and his behavior becomes more flexible and adaptive.

9

Automatic and
Deliberate Thought

From the discussion of the relationships among memories, abstractions, and predictions and the description of neuroprint hierarchies, we turn again to the consideration of the dynamics of thought. In this chapter, we will be concerned with two complementary matching procedures—automatic matching and deliberate matching—to describe two complementary thought modes: automatic thought and deliberate thought.

In chapter 8 it was said that "tighter fits" can be obtained between events and neuroprints, or between two neuroprints, at lower levels of the neuroprint hierarchy, and that when a tighter fit can be obtained it will be obtained. When a tighter fit is obtained, thought tends to proceed more automatically, thus less deliberately. *Automatic thought is the relatively rapid, involuntary proceeding of the matching process as the individual attempts to predict familiar events.*

When an event is predictable, the matching process tends to proceed automatically. Typically, a predictable event is quite familiar, and the individual has no trouble identifying it. In addition, he has little difficulty in predicting the event because it has been predicted often in the past. Thus, the matching process tends to proceed smoothly and rapidly, requiring little, if any, concentration on the part of the individual. Automatic thought involves the execution of reflexes and habits. As was indicated earlier, the autonomic functions of the body are governed by re-

Automatic and Deliberate Thought

flexes, which proceed automatically. Similarly, once habits are learned and practiced, and as long as events remain predictable, they are executed automatically.

Deliberate thought, or deliberation, is the relatively slow proceeding of the matching process as the individual attempts to predict an unfamiliar event, through ideation. Deliberate thought operates through ideation. When a prediction is being sought through deliberation, ideas are elicited and the individual is aware of the event to be predicted and the extent to which it matches the ideas being deliberated. Thus, in deliberation, the relationship between events and ideas is reviewed mentally.

It should be noted in passing that matching for identification is a basic term that refers to both automatic matching, which may occur without the awareness of the individual, and deliberate matching, which occurs with awareness. (The matching involved in both automatic and deliberate thought follows the matching model described in chapter 5.) When a match for identification occurs on the ideational level through deliberation, recognition of the event being deliberated occurs. That is, in deliberation, when a match is achieved between an event and a memory or an abstraction, an idea is elicited and the event is recognized.

The prediction of a novel event may be obtained through deliberation in one of two ways—through memorization or through abstraction. If the event is totally unfamiliar, it will need to be memorized because there are no neuroprints stored in the mind that match the event. The individual deliberates the event by concentrating on its features and studying the transitions that are taking place with the passage of time. As the event becomes recognizable and the transitions appear to be consistent, after continued study, the individual tends to predict the transitions from the initial appearance of the event. In this way deliberation results in the formation of ideas about totally unfamiliar events and allows the events to be recognized and predicted.

On the other hand, if some of the features of the novel event are familiar, deliberation will involve the matching of the familiar features with abstractions in search of a prediction. This application of deliberation permits the individual to preview in his mind the probability that one idea or another will lead to the confirmation of the prediction sought.

Galanter and Gerstenhaber posit a view that limits the definition of ideational thought much more than it is limited here, but their view highlights in a somewhat similar way the previewing of ideas in predicting events. They state that "Imaginal thinking is neither more nor less than constructing an image or model of the environment, running the model faster than the environment, and predicting that the environment will behave as the model does."[1]

The two applications of the deliberation process may operate in conjunction with each other as the individual attempts to predict a novel event. As a totally unfamiliar event is memorized so that some of its features become familiar, these features may then be matched with abstractions. The more features of the event become familiar through memorization, the more probable it becomes that they may be matched with abstractions.

Speed of thought is, of course, a relative matter. Automatic thought is faster than deliberate thought. But even within the domain of deliberate thought the process of previewing abstractions may produce predictions rather promptly, through insight, when compared to the laborious process of memorizing.

Automatic matching relies heavily on relating events to instincts and memories because it involves the execution of reflexes and habits; and reflexes are instinctive, while habits are most often based on memory. On the other hand, deliberate matching is quite often based on relating events to abstractions.

During deliberation, ideas can be reviewed and previewed in preparation for action. Although all thought is, in a sense, preparation for action, in deliberation alternative courses of action may be evaluated through abstraction before a decision for action is made. Or, to put it another way, in deliberation, action may be premeditated.

In contrast, when thought is automatic, the individual may not have a preconceived idea of the actions he is about to take. Thus,

[1] Eugene Galanter and Murray Gerstenhaber, "On Thought," p. 219.

automatic actions are often considered impulsive. Moreover, the individual may not even be aware of what he is doing.

The advantage in automatic matching is not only that it is faster than deliberation, but also that innumerable activities can be directed automatically at the same time—as, for example, the many autonomic functions of the body. If the individual attempts to deliberate too many events at the same time, he may easily become confused. In addition, accuracy sometimes depends on the speed of a response. For example, it is more difficult to draw a straight line slowly than rapidly. Finally, when individuals deliberate routine tasks that can be performed automatically, they often become bored and distracted, and errors may result.

On the other hand, deliberation may at times prove more accurate than automatic thought, because through the deliberation of abstractions alternatives may be considered before a course of action is embarked upon.

In chapter 8, I described how a greater tightness of fit in the matching process increases precision and therefore contributes to the accuracy of prediction. Consequently, a match will tend to be made at a lower level of the neuroprint hierarchy because greater correspondence can be achieved there. This suggests, further, that there is a tendency toward automatic thought because reflexes and habits prevail at the lower levels of the neuroprint hierarchy, and reflexes and habits are executed automatically.

The precision achieved in the matching process is one factor that contributes to the accuracy of prediction. Seeking tightness of fit—or a high degree of correspondence—to achieve precision may be considered as a vertical movement through the neuroprint hierarchy toward the lower levels.

Validity is another factor contributing to the accuracy of prediction. The search for validity may be considered as a horizontal movement across the categories of the neuroprint hierarchy. As one moves across the horizontal dimension of the neuroprint hierarchy, one encounters the categorization of different kinds of events. If, in attempting to predict an event, an individual does not achieve correspondence along the horizontal dimension, the resulting prediction will be inaccurate because he will not be predicting the prevailing event. That is, the resulting prediction would be invalid, therefore inaccurate, even if precision were achieved along the vertical dimension.

Let us return to the example concerning the eating of food. It was said in chapter 8 that an imprecise prediction could lead to the taking of poison. An invalid prediction could also lead in the following manner to the taking of poison. Presumably, "poison" and "food" would be categorized at different positions along the horizontal dimension that signified ingestion. If the individual were attempting to acquire food, but a match was made within the category "poison" instead of within the category "food," the resulting prediction would be invalid—therefore, inaccurate—and the individual would poison himself as a result.

The distinction between validity and precision can be illustrated in the following example. Suppose an individual is looking through a telescope in an attempt to make some predictions about the moon. If he is looking at the moon, the match will be valid; but if he is looking at Mars, the match will be invalid and the resulting predictions will also be invalid. Now, suppose he is making a valid match by focusing on the moon, but the telescope is out of focus, yielding a fuzzy, unclear view of the moon. He will not be able to achieve a match in any great detail. Therefore, the match will be imprecise, and the resulting prediction will tend to be inaccurate because of the imprecision of the match.

Both validity and precision contribute to the accuracy of prediction. If a match is invalid, it does not matter how precise it may be, because the wrong event is being predicted. If a match is imprecise, there is no tightness of fit, and the lack of correspondence will also effect the accuracy of prediction. This interpretation is consistent with the scientific interpretation of accuracy.

From this discussion, it should become clear that the comparison of alternatives through deliberation represents a search for validity. Of course, once the deliberation process has been engaged, precision may be estimated deliberately, too.

Automatic thought and deliberate thought are complementary

procedures; automatic thought is used to predict familiar events, while deliberate thought is used to predict unfamiliar or novel events. But there is something uniquely adaptive in the reciprocal relationship between these two thought processes. When events are being directed automatically and a mismatch occurs, denoting a novel situation, deliberation is initiated. Conversely, when an event has been deliberated sufficiently so that it has become familiar, it will subsequently be dealt with automatically by habit. Let me elaborate.

From what has been said in comparing the characteristics of automatic and deliberate thought, it should be clear that familiar events can be predicted automatically in a routine manner and predicting familiar events automatically is generally adaptive. So it appears that, in general, when events can be predicted automatically, they will be. But when events are being predicted automatically and a mismatch occurs, denoting a novel situation, arousal will increase and deliberation will be initiated.

When events are being matched with neuroprints automatically and a mismatch occurs, an "alerting discrepancy" is produced. Such a discrepancy causes the individual to become aware of the event, related ideational material is elicited, and the individual attempts to obtain a match between the event and ideas through deliberation. For this reason, only events that cannot be predicted automatically need be deliberated.

Once the deliberation of an event results in the formation of a neuroprint that allows the event to be predicted, if that event is subsequently predicted often, it will become familiar and will no longer need to be deliberated. Thereafter when the event appears, it will be dealt with automatically by habit. Automatic and deliberate thought here operate reciprocally to improve prediction.

If the matching process does not proceed automatically, it may be because either a match for identification or a match for prediction cannot be obtained automatically. If the event is not identified automatically, it must become identifiable through deliberation by means of memorization or by matching with an abstraction.

Once identification is achieved and matching for prediction

commences, if a prediction is not made automatically, the individual will attempt to predict the event through deliberation. By deliberating abstractions, he will try to determine a goal that can be predicted to reduce the arousal induced when identification occurs, and to determine a program predicted to lead to the goal. Deliberation for a prediction may involve a search for a goal, a program, or both. However, because individuals are aware more often of the goals they want to pursue (what they wish) than of the means of obtaining their goals, deliberation tends more often to involve a search for a program.

Some examples should clarify the relationship between automatic and deliberate thought. Let us first consider the relationship between reflexes—a type of automatic thought—and deliberation. The respiratory system is a reflexive system that operates automatically with only the peripheral awareness of the individual. When a mismatch occurs, however, arousal is generated and the event comes to his awareness. The inhaling subroutine of the breathing program probably is matched with the intake of oxygen. As long as oxygen is taken in when the inhaling subroutine of the breathing program is being executed, a match will occur, and the program will continue to operate smoothly and automatically. However, if a noxious gas is taken into the lungs while the inhaling subroutine is being executed, the individual may feel pain in his chest. Arousal is generated and the event is brought to his awareness for deliberation so that the predictability of the breathing program may be restored. As a result of deliberation, the noxious gas can be removed by proper procedures and the individual's normal breathing restored.

It is interesting to note that the neuroprints governing the autonomic functions of the body produce only scanty ideational material about the functions that they govern. As a result of this lack of knowledge, the individual may have difficulty in understanding the malfunction of his breathing apparatus when it occurs or how to remedy it. He may be aware that his breathing is labored, and he may experience a chest pain that suggests to him that the problem is in his chest. Many people have no knowledge of the internal breathing process, except for what they can infer from external signs such as the expansion and contraction of the chest. This is because the internal operations of most autonomic functions are not exposed for observation; therefore they cannot be learned. Unless a person learns how an autonomic function operates, he will not know.

Automatic matching also involves the execution of habits, which are inflexible programs that have been learned. When a habit is elicited by an event, it will tend to be executed automatically, as long as a match occurs between the progressive subroutines of the habit and the ensuing events. When a mismatch occurs, arousal will be generated and the unpredictable event will come to awareness, so that it may become predictable through deliberation.

To go back to the example offered earlier, if an individual becomes familiar with fanning an annoying fly away with his hand, a well-established master neuroprint will be developed in his mind, representing a habit. When a fly lands on him, he will begin to fan it away automatically, in rapid, coordinated movements, and with only peripheral attention. However, if the fly continues to disturb him, he may need to concentrate on it in order to remove it—that is, he may need to deliberate the problem. Assuming that he recognizes the creature as a fly and wishes to remove it, he will not need to deliberate either the event or the goal. His deliberation will involve the selection of another program that can be predicted to be more effective than the fanning action in removing the fly. He may then decide to use a fly swatter to remove the fly.

Because habits are learned initially through deliberation before they become habits, the individual has an idea of the operation of a habit. Thus, the effectiveness of the operation of a habit, such as swatting a fly away with one's hand, can be monitored on the ideational level. Consequently, a habit may be modified to achieve the intended outcome.

Conversely, because reflexes are innate and most often the individual is unaware of their operation, ideas about reflexes seldom develop, and consequently there is no basis for modifying the reflexes to make them more effective. When deliberation about a reflex occurs, it does so because the operation of a reflex has been observed and an idea portraying the reflex has developed.

The following example illustrates how automatic and deliberate thought may be related most efficiently. An individual learns to drive a car by deliberation. He learns to recognize and predict the events he may encounter. Certain events are learned at first through deliberation, in the hope that they may eventually be relegated to habit and executed automatically. The shifting of gears is one illustration. As the individual begins to learn how to shift gears through deliberation, he studies the route through the gear box and corrects his mistakes as he falters in his attempts to shift gears. With more and more practice, his gear shifting becomes smoother. It is then relegated to habit. This frees him to deliberate other problems, such as road and traffic conditions. Traffic conditions, unlike gear shifting, present the individual with so many new and dangerous problems that traffic cannot be dealt with entirely by habit. Problems involving gear shifting are not usually as frequent or as dangerous. When the individual is unable to shift gears by habit, the activities involved in gear shifting become unpredictable. As a result, they will be brought to awareness for deliberation. The individual might then move the car off the road to deliberate the gear-shifting problem.

Thus far I have attempted to characterize deliberate and automatic thought as complementary processes. When the matching process can proceed automatically, it will, but it can proceed automatically only when events are familiar. Deliberation begins when a mismatch occurs, signifying the emergence of a novel event that cannot be predicted automatically. If the event becomes predictable through deliberation and a habit is learned, the prediction of the event will subsequently occur automatically.

When events become unpredictable, deliberation will be directed toward the reinstatement of predictability above all else. Subordinate decisions may be made through the deliberation of abstractions, such as which of alternative goals one wishes to pursue or which of alternative programs one will select as the means of pursuing a given goal.

Automatic and Deliberate Thought

I am restating in this context what was said in chapter 3: Above all, the individual is motivated to maintain a predictable relationship with the environment. The maintenance of predictability is necessary in order for the individual to satisfy his needs and wants, whatever they may be. Once predictability is maintained, he may choose anything he wishes to pursue or any means of obtaining what he wishes.

I have said that I am in pursuit of an explanation of the excellence of human intelligence. It appears that at least two of the areas in which humans excel are their ability to understand alternatives and make choices and their ability to make predictions about the unfamiliar. If an individual's outlook were based solely on memory, his future would appear to be the same as his past. However, because of his ability to deliberate abstractions, he is not so circumscribed. He may speculate about events he has never encountered before and conceive of ways of experiencing them. It therefore seems that the development and deliberation of complex hierarchies of abstractions is the key to the superiority of human intelligence.

Moreover, humans find themselves in the state of too much predictability more often than do lower creatures, because humans more often can predict the means of their subsistence quickly and accurately. With little to challenge their confidence and time to spare, they can find life becoming monotonous. Humans are more often motivated to escape boredom by seeking novelty than are lower creatures. And the pursuit of novelty leads to the deliberation of abstractions, which in turn increases the probability of discovery and invention.

Yet the mind is seldom emphasized as a primary behavior determinant. I have attempted to show that the forces that determine behavior operate cyclically as parts of the feedback loop, and that the student of human behavior may enter the cycle at any point to investigate the force that is directing behavior at that juncture. If one enters the cycle where matching for identification occurs, one may be led to believe that the impinging stimulus is initiating behavior. However, if one enters the cycle where matching for prediction occurs—when abstractions are being deliberated to predict an unfamiliar event that is foreign to the individual's past experience—one can readily see how the mind operates as a primary determinant to initiate behavior.

In a sense, learning to identify an event may be regarded as the control of the mind by the events, because the appearance of the event seems to initiate identification; the mind is merely reacting. On the other hand, when the mind, through the deliberation of abstractions, generates predictions about events that have never been experienced before, and the individual confirms his predictions by creating an invention, the mind is initiating events, because the mind is conceiving a new experience. In this case, it may be contended, the mind is acting as a cause of events.

As proof of man's excellence, his ability to exercise volition is sometimes emphasized. Volition implies choice. The choice is made during the matching for prediction when the deliberation of abstractions results in the evaluation of alternative master neuroprints and the choice of one to direct action. Thus, a volitional act is the product of the deliberation of abstractions.

Intention is the rational state of mind that exists after a match for prediction is achieved and a program has been selected to pursue a goal. It can then be said that the individual intends to execute the program to achieve the goal. Recently, neurological research has begun to produce evidence that supports the existence of intentional behavior.[2]

Deliberation can be used with some latitude to memorize, preview, and review unfamiliar events in an effort to predict them. Thus, deliberation is not restricted to the prediction of current events. Deliberation may be concerned with the review of an event that the individual attempted to predict in the past, in the hope that it may be predicted more accurately or beneficially in the future should the need arise.

Deliberation may be extended over time to refine prediction. After a prediction has been tested and a feedback loop has been

[2] See, especially, D. M. McKay, "Cerebral Organization and the Conscious Control of Action"; H. Mittlestaedt, "Experience and Capacity"; H. L. Teuber, "Perception"; and W. Gray Walter, "Slow Potential Waves in Human Brain."

Automatic and Deliberate Thought

completed, new information can be sought to improve the accuracy of prediction. The recycling of the matching process in extended deliberation can continue until some desired degree of accuracy has been obtained.

Three factors contribute to man's excellence in predicting and controlling his environment.

• Man finds himself in a state of too much predictability more often than lower creatures. Therefore, he tends to pursue novelty more often, which increases the probability that he will make discoveries.

• Man has the potential for developing more complex hierarchies of abstractions than infrahumans. This gives him a greater potential for predicting the unknown and making discoveries.

• Societies provide information and methods for pursuing the unknown through instruction. This increases man's potential to make discoveries.

10

EMOTIONS

In this chapter, I shall attempt to explain emotion and its contribution to behavior, as interpreted within the context of my theory. Two mental functions are described in chapter 5: the arousal function, which was characterized as a diffuse and general intensity function, and the content function, which was described as a specific function that gives definition to experience. By indicating how emotion is related to both the arousal function and the content function of the mind, I hope to show that emotion is part of a unitary mental process, rather than a distinct and separate influence upon behavior.

The intensity of emotion is considered to be the intensity of feeling associated with arousal. As arousal increases, there is an increase in the intensity of feeling, which is regarded as an increase in the intensity of emotion.

The intensity of arousal indicates the degree of felt urgency and value of conceiving and confirming predictions. When arousal is low, the individual is in a relaxed or resting state. When arousal is moderate to high, the individual is alert, interested, and able to predict events. When arousal is excessive, the individual is disturbed and mentally unstable. Consequently, he is unable to predict and negotiate the environment effectively. Under these conditions the individual's ability to maintain a predictable relationship with the environment is threatened and he is compelled to restore mental stability so that he may predict and negotiate the environment effectively.

EMOTIONS

The relationship between the degree of arousal and the individual's ability to perform or negotiate the environment has been described by Malmo as follows: "The shape of the curve relating level of performance to level of activation [i.e., arousal] is that of an inverted U: from low activation up to a point that is optimal for a given performance or function, level of performance rises monotonically with increasing activation level; but past this optimal point the relation becomes nonmonotonic; further increase in activation beyond this point produces fall in performance level, this fall being directly related to the amount of the increase in level of activation."[1] It appears that there is a threshold level of arousal for a given individual, and that when the threshold level is exceeded, the individual's level of performance will begin to fall. As arousal increases beyond this threshold, the individual's performance will continue to fall.

It was stated in chapter 5 that the degree of predictability affects the level of arousal. Too much or too little predictability can generate excessive arousal, produce mental instability, and interfere with the individual's ability to predict and negotiate the environment. Man seeks an optimum level of predictability in his relationship with the environment. Optimum predictability occurs in a situation that includes enough novelty for the individual to extend his ability to predict and enough familiarity to permit him to make predictions that are required by the situation. Under these conditions arousal tends to be moderate to high, but not beyond the threshold level described by Malmo. When the individual is alert and actively negotiating the environment, he will find nuances challenging and manageable. But if there is either too little or too much predictability, arousal will become excessive, his mental process will become unstable, and he will attempt to restore mental stability.

When there is too much predictability, the individual becomes bored because there is too much sameness, and arousal will increase. Thus, boredom is a state of high arousal. In order to reduce arousal, the individual will seek enough novelty to eliminate the boredom of dealing with the monotonous stimulation. In extreme

[1] Robert B. Malmo, "Activation," p. 384.

boredom, the individual stops making predictions about the environment because they are unnecessary. The environment demands the same prediction over and over again, and so the individual needs to confirm only one prediction. This situation generates excessive arousal and mental instability. It should be mentioned, however, that when an individual is exhausted or fatigued, monotony will provide rest and lead to sleep. For instance, when a person is fatigued, he may count sheep to create monotony so that he may fall asleep. Under these conditions, sameness is quieting rather than arousing. But when the individual is alert and actively interested in predicting the environment, too much sameness is annoying to him.

When there is too little predictability, arousal increases because there is a pronounced incongruity between neuroprints and events. The environment seems strange and alien because the neuroprints in the mind do not match events. Arousal may be reduced by avoiding novelty and seeking familiar events that are easily predicted. In the extreme, too little predictability is confusing, arousal becomes excessive, and mental process becomes unstable.

For an individual who is alert and attempting to predict the environment, either too much or too little predictability will generate excessive arousal and mental instability. When his mind becomes unstable, his ability to maintain a predictable relationship with the environment is threatened. Consequently, he will direct his efforts toward maintaining a predictable relationship with the environment. When there is too much predictability, he will search for variety and novelty. When there is too little predictability, he will search for redundancy and familiarity. These compensatory reactions to either too much or too little predictability are directed toward stabilizing the mental process, so that the environment may be predicted and negotiated effectively.

The value an individual places on the selection and confirmation of predictions is positively correlated with the intensity of arousal or emotion that is generated at the time. The maintenance of predictability is valued above all else. When predictability is being maintained, the individual is able to attempt the prediction of specific events. The importance of predicting a specific event is determined initially at the time a match for identification is achieved and the individual becomes aware of the intensity of feeling he associates with the event. The more intense his feelings are, the more he will value the reduction of the intensity or arousal. When a match for prediction is achieved, arousal may increase or decrease, depending upon whether or not the reduction of arousal is predicted.

Arousal is closely associated with the survival instincts. It underlies the development of specific feelings and represents the intensity associated with specific feelings. However, specific feelings such as love cannot be thought of as opposite to arousal. A person's arousal level may be reduced if he is in love and is loved in return. Or his arousal level may be increased if he is in love and is not loved in return, or if he is jealous of a competitor.

Whether arousal represents the intensity of feeling associated with a specific event or is the kind of "free-floating" arousal that cannot be associated with a specific event, the degree of arousal determines the urgency and degree of value the individual imputes to the pursuit of a prediction. To clarify the relationship between arousal and events, let me analyze specific emotion

Emotion involves more than the intensity of feeling. I have said that ideas contain both the content of experiences and the feelings associated with the experiences. When an idea is elicited by an event, the idea generates an intensity of feeling that is associated with the event and an image of the event with which the feeling is associated. A specific emotion is not simply a greater amount of feeling; it is a recollection of the specific feelings about the particular events to which it is attached. An emotion can be identified only in terms of its content.

This implies that specific emotions are learned. At birth, specific situations, specific needs, and specific deficiencies (discrimination is necessary for the individual to realize that something is missing) are not mentally identifiable by an individual, even though the locus of the feeling may be identifiable objectively by others. For instance, I am not implying that hunger as a result of food deprivation is not specific, but that the ability of the individual to identify the feeling that occurs as a specific result of food deprivation as one that can be satisfied by food is the product of learning. If he cannot distinguish the feeling from other feelings and characterize it in terms of the conditions under which it arises, he cannot identify the emotion or feeling. The identification of an emotion depends upon the content of ideas.

The mind of the newborn infant contains few ideas. Therefore, the infant's feelings are relatively undifferentiated and are characterized mainly by the variations in their intensity rather than in content. As the infant learns to associate his feelings with an increasing number of specific events, his inventory of ideas becomes more differentiated and so do his feelings. This is a refining and differentiating process that changes the individual's amorphous feelings of early childhood to more graded and distinct feelings as he matures. Thus, at any given stage of his maturity, his feelings become more modulated and more distinct than at an earlier, less differentiated stage.

Moreover, as the individual matures, there is a decreased probability that he will have extreme reactions to events. This is not to say that the adult is incapable of extreme emotions. But since more-graded reactions are learned as the individual matures, it is more probable that an event will elicit a more modulated reaction in a more mature person.

Once a match for identification has been achieved and the individual becomes aware of the initiating event and the feelings he associates with it, his feelings are specific because he is aware of the conditions from which his feelings arise. Subsequently, when a match for prediction is achieved, his feelings about the event become even more specific because not only is he aware of the conditions which give rise to his feelings but, in addition, he may be aware of the specific goal that will reduce arousal and satisfy his feelings. For instance, emotions are more specific when the individual knows not only that he is hungry but also that food will satisfy his hunger.

When a match for prediction is achieved, the goal portrayed by the master neuroprint that is elicited may involve either seeking or avoiding a specific event. When the content of the master neuroprint indicates that arousal will be reduced if an event is achieved, the event will have positive value for the individual.

EMOTIONS

On the other hand, if the content of the master neuroprint indicates that arousal will be reduced by avoiding an event, the event will have negative value. Thus, it is the content of the neuroprint that indicates whether an event will have positive or negative value.

For example, if the individual is hungry, the acquisition of food will be predicted to alleviate arousal, and he will seek food; the stimulus—food—is positively valued. But if the individual is sitting close to a hot fire and the heat causes excessive arousal, an idea will be stimulated which will predict that moving away from the heat will reduce arousal. In this case, the fire is imputed to have negative value, and avoidance behavior will be indicated. An environmental object is assigned positive value when the acquisition of it is predicted by the content of an idea to reduce excessive arousal; an object is assigned negative value when the avoidance of the object is predicted to reduce excessive arousal.[1]

Positive emotion is primarily associated with low arousal, which denotes relaxation, and with the prediction that excessive arousal may either be reduced or prevented. Negative emotion is associated primarily with excessive arousal and with the inability either to predict its reduction or the prevention of its intensification.

The individual becomes disoriented and unable to predict when arousal becomes excessive whether his feelings are positive or negative. Extremely euphoric states of mind, such as those that are produced by certain drugs, are as destructive to prediction as extremely depressive states. In both extreme depression and extreme euphoria, the individual is unable to predict and deal with the environment.

I have described emotion as part of a unitary mental process. The input that leads to the formation of neuroprints may be distinguished in terms of general arousal and specific content. However, the ideas that are projected after a neuroprint forms

[1] Although most problems in predicting are associated with excessively high arousal, a few problems are associated with excessively low arousal. For instance, arousal may be excessively low after taking an overdose of tranquilizers. Such problems are remedied by finding a way to increase arousal. In this case, the individual might value drinking numerous cups of coffee.

tend to blend content and arousal together, so that although the individual may try to distinguish what is happening—that is, the content of an experience—from his feelings about the experience, he will find it difficult to discuss the content without injecting his feelings or to discuss his feelings without referring to content.

Of course, it is possible to represent content alone—say, in the drawing of a picture of a collie (i.e., the features of a collie). However, a child who is exposed to the picture will not only learn that it is a collie, he will also attach his feelings about dogs to the experience, so that the idea that forms in his mind will represent both a collie in terms of its content and his feelings about the collie based upon his ideas about dogs.

Perhaps progress in the study of behavior has been restricted because we tend to separate aspects of mental operations. The Freudian terms *id, ego,* and *superego* represent a case in point. The more general dichotomizing of the psyche into intellect and affect is another example. Compartmentalizing the mind in these ways can lead to some serious problems and to confusion in the interpretation of mental process.

For example, viewing the individual as primarily motivated toward pleasure may suggest that the feeling of pleasure is the goal or end of behavior and that the content of ideas provides the means to that end. Usually, the differentiation between means and ends is ambiguous. It depends upon the perspective of the observer as he looks at a series of events. The distinction between means and ends becomes fallacious when content is defined as representing the means and a state of feeling, the end. This becomes evident when one considers that any idea of an outcome contains both content and the feeling the individual associates with it, and that any event selected as a means of reaching the outcome will contain content as well as the feeling attached to it. Thus, both the means and the end are selected on the basis of the implications of the content and the feeling the individual associates with it. Besides, the more pleasurable event may not be the one most preferred—for instance, if the individual believed that the more pleasurable event could not be achieved.

EMOTIONS

It seems accurate, then, to say that, after evaluating the content and feelings associated with relevant neuroprints, the individual expresses a preference in making a selection of a master neuroprint to direct behavior. He evaluates the content of neuroprints in considering such substantive matters as the probability of achieving a given goal by means of a given program. Thus, the content of ideas indicates whether the achievement of events, and the programs necessary for achieving them, can be predicted. The individual evaluates the feelings associated with neuroprints in considering how he may feel as a given program directs him toward a goal as well as how he may feel when the goal has been achieved.

The term *preference* seems especially appropriate in reference to the selection of a master neuroprint to direct behavior after alternative ideas have been considered through the deliberation of abstractions. When both the content of various ideas and the feelings associated with them have been deliberated and a choice is made, the result is not merely the expression of a wish for a pleasurable experience; the result is an expression of a preference for a course of action that is predictable as well as pleasure-giving —but above all, predictable. Predictability is important because the individual must be able to maintain a predictable relationship with the environment to gratify his wishes—whatever they may be.

Let us now examine how internal and external states become related in the formation of master neuroprints.

The arousal function appears to monitor the internal states of the individual—that is, it monitors the internal signals (chemical reactions) that compose the stimuli of internal events. The content function defines the specific sources of the arousal that emanate from both internal and environmental events. Internal and external events become related in a master neuroprint when an external event is predicted to reduce the arousal attached to an internal event.

For instance, when a person becomes hungry, the reduction of nutrients in the blood elicits, during the process of matching for identification, the neuroprint representing hunger, which in turn projects the idea of hunger at some degree of intensity. The intensity of the hunger is cued by the arousal function. The content function of the mind identifies the experience that is generating the arousal as hunger by the specific sensations accompanying the event—a feeling of emptiness in the stomach, perhaps an increased sensitivity of the taste buds, and increased salivation. It is through the process of ideation that the individual is able to recognize that he is hungry. The neuroprint representing the idea of hunger is then refined through a more detailed definition of the content of the neuroprint as the individual becomes increasingly aware of the events that discriminate hunger from other internal events that generate arousal, such as thirst or sexual excitation.

When the individual learns that food reduces hunger, a neuroprint representing food forms in his mind and becomes associated with the neuroprint representing hunger in the formation of a master neuroprint. Because he has learned that an external event such as food reduces the arousal associated with an internal event such as hunger, he imputes value to the external event. Subsequently, when there is a lowering of nutrients in his blood, the neuroprint projecting the idea of hunger (at some degree of intensity) will be elicited to constitute a match for identification. Then, assuming that there is sufficient arousal, a match for prediction will be sought, and the master neuroprint displaying the transition from hunger to the acquisition of food as a means of reducing the arousal will be elicited, generating the prediction that the acquisition of food will reduce the hunger. It is in such a way that master neuroprints mediate between internal and external states.

The mediation of master neuroprints between internal and external states and the predictions that become possible as a result enable the individual to tolerate delay and to become satisfied before external conditions have provided sufficient substances to restore the internal chemical imbalance that generated arousal initially. Let us suppose that the reduction of nutrients in the individual's blood projects the idea of a degree of hunger; subsequently, there is placed before him an amount of food that he predicts will satisfy that degree of hunger. His prediction may tend to reduce arousal even before he begins to eat, and he may be able to tolerate some delay before eating. His hunger may also subside temporarily even though he has not eaten enough food for the nutrients in his blood to be restored above the chemical level that initiated the transmission of hunger cues in the first place. These reactions can occur because the individual is able to predict the eating of a sufficient amount of food to satisfy his hunger.

Once such a master neuroprint is formed, portraying the relationship between hunger and food, variations on the initial conception—in this example, that food satisfies hunger—may develop. These variations define the many relationships between food and hunger that can be learned. For instance, a related neuroprint may develop that initiates the prediction that the appearance of food will cause hunger—that is, the person learns that the sight of food will make him hungry. This variation is, in essence, a reversal of the initial prediction. For this reason a person on a reducing diet may not wish to watch other people eat.

A master neuroprint may also define an autistic means of reducing an internal state of arousal, one that does not depend on the acquisition of anything from the environment, although the autistic mode may, at times, be regarded as a substitution for an environmental encounter. For example, a lowering of nutrients in the blood may cue the idea of hunger (matching for identification), which may in turn elicit the master neuroprint that portrays that hunger may be satisfied through thumb sucking (matching for prediction). As a result, the individual may suck his thumb to reduce arousal. Or the master neuroprint elicited when a match for prediction is sought may indicate that fantasizing about the eating of food can be predicted to reduce hunger. In this case, the individual may think about food to reduce his hunger. In the first example, autonomous action (thumb sucking) is used to placate hunger; in the second example, hunger is placated strictly within the ideational framework. There are many other autistic modes of reducing arousal, which will be discussed further in the following chapter, when restorative defenses are discussed.

11

DEFENSIVENESS

It has been noted that when there is either too much or too little predictability for extended periods, arousal becomes excessive, the individual's mental process becomes unstable, and he is unable to predict and negotiate the environment effectively. Under these conditions compensatory reactions are engaged so that the individual may be able to maintain a predictable relationship with the environment and predict events effectively.

If there is too much predictability while the individual is alert and active, a compensatory seeking of variation and novelty is generated to escape boredom. Because the events are monotonously redundant, the individual has difficulty determining the predictions that are required by the events, and the environment provides little basis for the testing of predictions. Under these conditions mental process becomes unstable.

The popularity of television may be attributed in part to the pursuit of variety and novelty. Adventure is available to the individual at the turn of a switch, and if he becomes bored with a particular program, he can change channels. The mountain climber's explanation that he climbs mountains "because they are there" may also be understood in part by considering it from this perspective. The suspense and surprise in the plot of any comedy or tragedy offer playgoers and movie viewers the element of novelty and adventure, which helps to account in part for the appeal of plays and movies and other forms of diversion such as sports, games, and puzzles. Why people seek entertainment can be explained in part in terms of the opportunity such amusements present for the individual to escape too much predictability and to extend his scope of prediction.

On the other hand, if there is too little predictability, compensatory reactions will be directed toward redundancy and familiarity so that a match may be achieved between neuroprints and events. When there is a pronounced mismatch, the environment seems alien and confusing, and the person's mental process becomes unstable. This may explain in part why people retreat in some situations to routine and rituals, and why children cling to "security blankets."

In the extreme, too much or too little predictability produces mental instability and unpredictability. A compensatory reaction to too much or too little predictability is defensiveness. However, life is so full of novelty that the boredom imposed by too much predictability can usually be overcome with a little effort. Too much predictability, therefore, seldom becomes so pronounced and prolonged that it generates mental instability. Ordinary circumstances induce too little predictability much more often. In general, from birth onward, the individual struggles to gain more and more predictability. For this reason, defensiveness is more commonly associated with too little predictability.

Defensiveness may be defined as the "filtering out" or ignoring of environmental stimulation for the purpose of reducing arousal and mental instability, so that the individual may predict and negotiate the environment effectively. When there is too little predictability and the individual becomes defensive, he ignores variable and novel events. When there is too much predictability and the individual becomes defensive, he ignores redundant and familiar events.

Defensiveness is adaptive in that it contributes to the maintenance of a predictable relationship with the environment by stabilizing mental process and, therefore, preparing the individual to make specific predictions effectively. On the other hand, defensiveness is maladaptive, because in the process certain environmental stimuli are ignored. Thus, defensiveness falsifies experience, which in turn interferes with the individual's ability to predict events.

The effect of defensiveness on adaptation can be understood if one realizes that it is necessary to maintain mental stability before it is possible to predict specific events. The maintenance of mental stability, then, is prerequisite to the accurate prediction of any specific event.

There are two general modes of defensive thought: thought directed toward the prevention of mental instability and thought directed toward the restoration of mental stability. Prevention is initiated to avert the disorientation and unpredictability that accompanies the mental instability the individual anticipates.

Preventive defensiveness is initiated before arousal reaches the level of panic and the individual becomes disoriented. At the time preventive defensiveness is initiated, the individual is still able to negotiate the environment.

When too much predictability is anticipated, preventive defensiveness involves ignoring familiar events that have become monotonous and pursuing novel events to escape boredom and prevent mental instability. For example, an individual performing a monotonous job on a factory production line may defensively attempt to escape boredom by ignoring the routine tasks he is performing and by seeking nuances in the environment. The defensive filtering out of the demands of his repetitive task to prevent the mental instability he anticipates falsifies events, which in turn increases the probability of an accident.

When too little predictability is anticipated, preventive defensiveness involves ignoring novel stimulation that has become confusing and pursuing familiar events that are readily predictable. Mental process is directed to ensure that the next prediction will be confirmed. Suppose, for example, that a person has been thwarted in numerous love affairs. Because of his past experiences, he will tend to predict that he will be thwarted in a subsequent affair. On the other hand, he would prefer to be loved. According to the theory, if he anticipates unpredictability, he will arrange his relationship with the environment to confirm the prediction that he will be thwarted—at the sacrifice of promoting that which he prefers, love and affection—because he believes that this prediction will be confirmed. Moreover, to prevent unpredictability from occurring, he will attempt to confirm the prediction that he will be thwarted. He may become overposssessive or overaggressive because he is anticipating the loss of love and affection once more. As a result, he is likely to confirm his prediction that he will be unloved in the future as he has been in the past because the defensive program selected to maintain predictability will steer his behavior toward this outcome, an outcome that is not too difficult for him to achieve. Thus, he is able to maintain predictability at the expense of achieving love.

Characteristic of preventive defensiveness against too little predictability is the vicious circle of defensive behavior, which involves a ritualistic, repeated employment of a well-established program to prevent unpredictability. Whenever an unpredictable stimulation emerges, the defensive individual attempts to prevent unpredictability at the expense of achieving his preferences. Consequently, he will neither learn to acquire his preferences nor improve his ability to predict.

The programs employed in such preventive defensiveness are likely to represent primitive programs, which are remnants of early childhood, because primitive programs are well established and easy to execute successfully. For this reason, such defensiveness is generally regressive in nature.

An interesting explanation emerges in the analysis of preventive defensiveness, the explanation of why some people are inclined toward failure. In general, failure is easier to confirm than success, as I have suggested in the example above. When an individual finds that events are becoming too unpredictable, he will attempt to confirm his next prediction. Because a prediction of failure is usually easier to confirm than a prediction of success, he will tend to predict failure and will act to achieve this outcome so as to confirm the failure he has predicted.

When the individual's preventive efforts fail and unpredictability occurs for any extended period of time, he will become disoriented and unable to negotiate the environment. In addition, his arousal will have exceeded the threshold level mentioned previously and he will be in a state of excessive arousal. In this state of mind, he will resort to defensive modes of thought to restore his mental stability and his ability to predict and negotiate the environment. He will tend to ignore external stimulation and resort to an autonomous mode of restoring predictability. Such a defensive mode of thought is autistic.

In chapter 5, I defined autism as an idea and/or program that operates divorced from environmental events. Let me cite, first, an example of autism representing too little predictability and then an example of autism representing too much predictability.

If the individual is aroused by hunger, and panic is induced before he is able to acquire food from the environment, he may suck his thumb for temporary relief or fantasize about eating food. In the case of thumb sucking, the autistic mode that is employed involves the operation of a motor program. Fantasizing represents an ideational autistic mode. Both are examples of autism generated when there is too little predictability.

Although the individual is seldom placed in a situation in which too much predictability is so prolonged that mental process becomes unstable and events become unpredictable, a prisoner's reaction to "Chinese water torture" (constant dripping of water on a person's forehead) provides an example of mental instability induced through monotonously redundant stimulation. We have also been provided insights into reactions to too much sameness through research that involves the imposition of "white noise" on subjects for extended periods.

In the case of too little predictability, autism will be directed toward creating familiar stimulation. In the case of too much predictability, autism will be directed toward the creation of novelty. These autistic activities are means of reducing arousal without relying on the environment. In essence, what happens in the matching process when autism becomes the mode of reducing arousal is that a match for prediction is achieved between the neuroprint of the event inducing arousal and a master neuroprint that portrays a means of reducing the arousal autonomously. So, for example, when panic results because the individual is unable to acquire food from the environment, a master neuroprint may be elicited that directs thumb sucking or fantasizing about eating.

An autistic activity is usually a substitute for satisfaction that may be gained from the environment. It often provides only temporary relief; to seek substantive relief, the individual will need to become involved with the environment again when his mental stability has been restored. For example, thumb sucking and fantasizing about eating are at best a temporary psychological substitute for eating. These activities are adaptive only because they restore mental stability so that the individual is able to deal with the environment again.

All forms of autism attempt to restore mental stability in order to enable the individual to relate effectively to the environment. Autism is, therefore, adaptive, even though an individual in an extended state of autism is insane. Insanity may be regarded as a prolonged, desperate, and final attempt to restore predictability. As such, insanity is an attempt to adapt. While an insane person is in a psychotic episode, autism has not yet been effective in reducing arousal sufficiently to enable him to relate to the environment.

Autism is a defense, and the insanity it may generate may be regarded as defensive insanity. It should be acknowledged, however, that there is a type of insanity that may be a result of defenselessness. Defenseless insanity results from the individual's inability to utilize defenses to stabilize mental process. It is associated with a dysfunction of the defensive operation of the mind. Environmental input is admitted indiscriminately, and the individual is unable to predict it.

Defensiveness is maladaptive because it falsifies experience. Ignoring either novel or familiar stimulation prevents the individual from dealing with the events that are upon him. Any predictions that he makes will be based on incomplete information. Hence, they will probably be inaccurate. In preventive defensiveness involving too little predictability, it is as if the individual is pretending that events are familiar when they may not be, because he attends only to those familiar stimuli that he may most assuredly predict. In restorative defensiveness, external stimulation is more completely ignored. It is as if the individual is temporarily forsaking an errant environment in favor of an imagined world that is more predictable.

Defensive modes of thought are often unsucessful in maintaining predictability. Thus, they often do not acomplish their purpose. If a novel stimulation is a threat and the individual engages in preventive defensiveness, he will tend to ignore the novel stimulation. But not all stimulation can be ignored. The unpredictable stimulus may continue to plague him in spite of his efforts to ignore it, and, as a result, his arousal may continue to increase. When excessive arousal occurs, autism may be employed as a restorative defense to reduce it, but the event that caused the panic may not relent and the individual cannot ignore it.

It is important to stress that defensiveness is maladaptive because it falsifies environmental events, thereby impairing prediction. But this should not be interpreted to mean that all pretense is maladaptive. When pretense is a preparation for predicting the environment and does not involve defensiveness, it may indeed be adaptive. The play of young children can be an adaptive preparation for life. Pretending in the existence of Santa Claus may be adaptive because it prepares children to engage in altruistic exchanges with others. The belief in Santa Claus does not represent an autistic retreat from the environment; rather, it is an idea that contains learning that may be transferred to help children relate to others constructively. In short, pretending can help to develop adaptive ideas. As Bruno Bettelheim says, "If we really want our children to develop a healthy understanding and mastery of reality we must make it possible for them to enjoy their childhood fantasies."[1]

Defensiveness against too little predictability primarily involves automatic matching. The individual tends to ignore the novel and attempts to predict the familiar automatically. On the other hand, defensiveness against too much predictability involves defensive deliberation. The individual tends to ignore the familiar and deliberates the novel excessively.

---

[1] "Dialogue with Mothers," p. 15.

The preventive defenses of early childhood tend to be automatic because the young child, confronted with a complex world he must learn to predict, tends to learn defenses against too little predictability. Such defenses direct behavior toward the prediction of familiar events because they are more easily predicted, and familiar events tend to be predicted automatically.

Primitive defenses based on too little predictability tend to become permanent because deliberation tends to be bypassed when they are employed. It was said that deliberation is employed to predict the unfamiliar. However, when a situation arises that generates defensiveness involving too little predictability, the novel aspects of the situation are not deliberated—they are shut out or ignored—and the most familiar elements of the situation are predicted automatically. This suggests a reason why defensive modes of thought operate without awareness. When deliberation is bypassed in this way, the unfamiliar features of a situation involving defensiveness tend to be ignored repeatedly and, therefore, remain unpredictable.

In a sense, then, defensiveness short circuits the adaptive relationship between automatic and deliberate thought. This is unfortunate, because an unpredictable situation that is traumatic for a child and results in defensiveness might easily be predicted when the child is older, if the unfamiliar aspects of the situation could be deliberated.

Although early defensiveness tends to be automatic, once the individual matures and becomes artful at deliberation, deliberation can be used defensively. With maturity, the individual gains mastery in predicting the environment, which in turn predisposes him to encounter the same situations repeatedly. This may lead to boredom and defensive deliberation. Moreover, when automatic defensiveness is used repeatedly, it becomes ritualized and contributes to boredom, resulting in the probable employment of defensive deliberation.

In addition, when the mode of defense proceeds automatically, it results in impulsive actions that are carried over from childhood. These actions often constitute behavior that is not acceptable in an adult and that frequently leads to undesirable consequences. The adult may thereupon become afraid to act and may try to defend against his own impulsive actions by engaging in excessive deliberation. Such an adult tends to be obsessive. For him, the effectiveness of deliberation as a means of weighing alternatives before acting is lost, because he overdeliberates as a defense against action and consequently tends to be chronically indecisive. Although he will repeatedly contemplate the unfamiliar, his deliberations will be inconsequential because they will not lead to action. Most probably, the actions he does take after such excessive deliberation will be a result of regressive automatic matching.

I have been describing defensive avoidance by thought, which is maladaptive because it does not allow the individual to improve his ability to predict. Defensive avoidance by action, however, is not necessarily maladaptive. Let us consider avoidance by both thought and action to make the comparison.

Ideally, the individual will seek novel events to expand his ability to predict, and he will attempt to acquire his preferences. This will lead him to attempt to control the situations he encounters, because by controlling events he becomes their master and can do with them what he wishes. If an event is to some extent unpredictable, he will fail to control it as he wishes. He will then attempt to predict it sufficiently to be able to avoid it if it should become a threat—that is, he will attempt to control his relationship with the event so that he might avoid it should the need arise. This consitutes the ability to avoid a potential threat through action, which requires some ability to predict the threat. Avoidance by action is adaptive—as, for instance, in the ability to predict and carry out a program for the avoidance of a hurricane. Moreover, while the person is avoiding the threat he may attempt to conceive of ways to extend his control over it in the future.

On the other hand, if the individual engages in defensive thought against too little predictability in the face of a threat, he will shut out or disregard errant, unpredictable characteristics of the event. This may prevent him from avoiding it effectively and preclude him from conceiving of a way of dealing with it in the future. As he defensively attempts to prevent unpredictability from occurring, by disregarding the unfamiliar aspects of the event, he is preventing himself from being able to predict the event; he is, in effect, burying his head in the ground like an ostrich.

A young child cannot distinguish between the consequences of thought and the consequences of action. He tends to feel that thinking about something bad has the same consequences as doing something bad. However, action elicits consequences from the environment. Thought does not. There need be only one consequence of thought, and that is action.[2] The defensive individual is not able to deliberate effectively. He is unable to consider, before he acts, the various possible consequences of his actions and to act in accordance with such deliberation.

The more mature individual who has experience deliberating effectively is able to preview events before deciding on a course of action and to select a program to direct his actions on the basis of his deliberation. Such an individual is aware that thought may precede and provide an effective basis for action.

Defensiveness helps to prepare the individual to predict and negotiate the environment. There are other mental states that are a part of the preparatory process but that do not falsify experience as defensiveness does. These include mental states of relaxation, such as sleeping or reminiscing. Such mental states preserve mental stability by reducing fatigue and providing diversion from the work of conceiving and validating predictions. Reminiscing involves the review of past experiences as a pleasurable pastime, without the need to predict.

The following outline of the various divisions and subdivisions of thought that have been described will help to place my theory in perspective. The outline highlights the focus of the theory and

---

[2] It should be acknowledged that when an action is taken, the thought that led to the action may be considered in determining the consequences that shall be invoked for the act. For example, the consequences are more severe for premeditated murder than for unpremeditated murder.

shows systematically the relationships between the parts of the theory and the whole.

   I. Thought directed toward the conception and confirmation of specific predictions
     A. Automatic thought
       1. Reflexive matching
       2. Habit
     B. Deliberate thought
       1. Memorizing
       2. Deliberation of abstractions
         a. Insight
         b. Evaluation of alternatives
  II. Thought directed toward the stabilization of mental process in preparation for the effective prediction of specific events
     A. Defensiveness
       1. Automatic defensive thought
         a. Preventive defensive thought
         b. Restorative defensive thought
       2. Defensive deliberation
     B. Relaxation
       1. Reminiscing
       2. Pretending

The theory attempts to focus on and explain rational behavior. It was said in chapter 1 that the individual is behaving rationally when he is conceiving predictions about observable events and testing them through observation. It can be seen that, of the various thought modes presented in the outline above, rational thought is restricted to the types of thought included under roman numeral one—that is, thought directed toward the conception and confirmation of specific predictions. When the individual is behaving rationally, he is able to participate with the environment in order to conceive and confirm predictions about specific environmental events.

The thought modes listed under roman numeral two are concerned with the preparation of mental process for rational thought and behavior—that is, with the stabilization of mental process so

DEFENSIVENESS

that the individual may be able to conceive and confirm predictions effectively about specific environmental events. These
thought modes are discussed in this book primarily because they
affect rational thought and behavior, but they are not the central
focus of the theory.

PART III / SOME IMPLICATIONS OF
THE THEORY

12

Individual Adjustment

The theory I have presented in the previous chapters focuses on the behavior of the individual. In this chapter, I will deal with one of the important implications of the theory, the explanation of individual adjustment. Within the context of the theory, the criterion for individual adjustment is the ability to predict accurately. The well-adjusted individual, then, is one who is able to predict accurately and who seeks encounters with the environment to improve his ability to predict. Any obstruction to his ability to predict will lead to maladjustment, while any condition that promotes accurate prediction will promote adjustment.

However, an individual who may be considered well adjusted will be able to predict accurately only to a certain degree, and an individual who may be considered maladjusted will be able to make at least some accurate predictions, unless he is totally insane. For this reason, I shall attempt to characterize the behavior of a well-adjusted individual as a type in contrast to that of a maladjusted individual—in other words, I shall attempt to define the characteristics of an individual who predicts accurately a good portion of the time as opposed to those of a person who predicts inaccurately.

Let us begin by considering the well-adjusted person, one who is able to maintain a predictable relationship with the environment. Because of his ability to predict, the well-adjusted individual tends to be self-confident. Such an individual has developed

SOME IMPLICATIONS OF THE THEORY

self-confidence because he has been able to maintain a predictable relationship with his environment in the past and is therefore confident that he will be able to predict accurately in the future. In the process of maintaining a predictable relationship with the environment, the self-confident individual has been largely successful in achieving his preferences and has gradually extended his scope of prediction. He tends not be to defensive. His confidence in his ability to predict causes him to seek novel stimuli and to regard them as a challenge. He does not consider new experiences a threat and does not defensively attempt to shut them out.

The self-confident individual can tolerate specific unpredictable occurrences because he feels certain that he can predict enough of the environment to achieve satisfaction when he chooses. In fact, he may seek unpredictable stimulation to escape boredom, but he must return to deal with aspects of the environment that he has already mastered to secure at least the necessities of life. He is likely to find attempts to predict the novel interesting and challenging rather than threatening, although his confidence could be undermined if the predictions upon which it is based suddenly became invalid. If this should happen, he will try desperately to reinstate predictability, by studying the novel environmental stimulation and deliberating abstractions in search of a prediction. He will not easily panic or resort to flights of fantasy.

The self-confident individual can tolerate not only unpredictability but also delay. The confidence he has in his ability to formulate predictions and to confirm them permits him to take time to deliberate novel stimulation and to pursue without desperation the programs that are produced by his deliberation.

To the extent that a person has become expert in predicting within a given area of interest or competence, he is correspondingly coolheaded when confronted with new challenges in that field. The expert race driver, for instance, may experience a rise in arousal during performance, since he is well aware of the risks and hazards involved, but this is not the same as the disabling panic the novice experiences.

As a practical matter, we often judge an individual's intellectual and technical competence in some given area not by a precise testing of his knowledge but by observing the degree of aplomb and the lack of excitement he exhibits in that area. In fact, this is how the amateur—say, the patient in a doctor's office—judges the professional; the substantive basis for these "intuitive" judgments of professional competence is certainly derived from the dependable relation between coolheadedness and knowledge of the matters at hand.

Autonomy has often been used as an index of personal adjustment. From this viewpoint, it is contended that maturation proceeds from total dependence toward autonomy, and that when the individual becomes autonomous, he is well adjusted. If autonomy is regarded as the ability to control the sources of one's satisfaction with minimum assistance from others, as it often is, the degree of an individual's autonomy is an inadequate index of adjustment. Self-confidence does not require autonomy; it requires the ability to predict. Therefore, an individual may be well adjusted without being autonomous—that is to say, he may be self-confident, without being able to control the sources of his own satisfaction, as long as he can predict that others will provide satisfaction for him. Moreover, there is reason to believe that if a person does not develop self-confidence in early childhood, when autonomy is impossible, his chances of becoming a relatively autonomous adult may be substantially impaired.

The infant has very little control over his own satisfaction and must depend upon adults to minister to his needs. To ensure his survival, he must rely on the simple signs and symbols he can express to communicate his needs to ministering adults. Nevertheless, he will feel secure and will gain self-confidence if his requests are granted by adults in spite of his lack of autonomy.

It seems, then, that it is not the individual's ability to control his relationship with the environment that builds his self-confidence but, rather, his ability to predict accurately. Autonomy seems to be imposed upon the individual rather than sought by him. All societies require an increasing degree of autonomy of the individual as he grows older. Thus, the push toward autonomy appears to be more external than internal, especially when one considers the individual's propensity to surrender autonomy for dependence, as Erick Fromm made eminently clear in his book *Escape from Freedom*. He explains how demagogues rise to power, because people are willing to surrender their freedom to be taken care of by a strong father surrogate.

Now let us examine some aspects of the individual who is maladjusted. In general, it may be said that the individual who is maladjusted lacks self-confidence, lacks self-esteem, and feels insecure because he has little confidence in his ability to predict. His lack of confidence is based on his past inability to maintain a predictable relationship with his environment. This, in turn, causes him to fear and anticipate unpredictability in the future. For this reason he tends to be involved in defensive thought for a substantial portion of the time. Such an individual may be said to suffer from a fear of the unknown. He regards the world as alien and dangerous. When his lack of self-confidence becomes pronounced, he will tend to be pessimistic and despondent and to feel worthless.

A person who lacks self-confidence cannot tolerate experiences that generate a high degree of negative emotion because they imply that his relationship with the environment might soon become unpredictable again and cause him to become panic-stricken. In contrast to the self-confident individual, the insecure person finds boredom a refuge from the constant need to bear negative emotions and the threat of unpredictability that it poses for him. He spends much of his time defending against unpredictability instead of being concerned about his preferences or extending his scope of prediction and control. Such persistent involvement in defensive thought tends to make his encounters with the environment even more unpredictable, because defensiveness falsifies experience.

Although defensiveness helps to prevent and reduce the immediate panic that results from unpredictability, its excessive use generally will prevent the individual from improving his ability to predict, thus increasing the probability that he will panic in the long run. Individuals who are unable to maintain a predictable relationship with the environment become overinvolved in states of autism. Their involvement in euphoric states of fantasy—such as are produced by alcohol and certain drugs, for instance—may become customary, as they seek or attempt to prolong such a state so as to escape what they perceive as an alien environment. Although all of us tend to escape, at times, from the burdens of predicting the environment, we expect to return to our daily chores at a predetermined time; an occasional escape—as in vacations or flights of fun and fancy—does not render our relationship with the environment less predictable.

The inability to predict leads to defensiveness, and the excessive use of defenses is a manifestation of maladjustment and perhaps of mental illness. Although the topic of mental illness is not a central issue of the proposed theory, the theory does suggest some explanations of mental illness. Let us see how the theory applies to different degrees of mental illness, ranging from insanity to less severe cases, which I shall refer to as mental disturbance.

An episode of insanity is generally regarded as a break with reality. According to the theory I have advanced, the break results after repeated attempts to predict the environment have failed and arousal has risen to the level of panic. The individual then turns his attention inward, away from the unpredictable environment, in an effort to reduce his mental instability through some autistic means and consequently be able to predict his environment once again. From this perspective, insanity is seen as involving dissociation from the environment and indulgence in autism for the purpose of restoring one's ability to predict the environment. An individual becomes insane to escape encounters with the environment so that he may restore his ability to predict. Insanity is a final, desperate effort to regain predictability and therefore may be regarded as adaptive.

The mentally disturbed individual engages less in restorative defenses and more in preventive defenses; thus, he engages less in autism and detachment from reality. Since preventive defenses involve the individual in conceiving and testing predictions against environmental feedback, a person engaged in preventive defenses is in touch with reality, whereas one engaged in restorative defenses is not. Moreover, the individual employing preventive defenses is attempting to guard against anticipated panic and the necessity to resort to restorative defenses.

The problem with preventive defenses is that the insecure individual tends continually to anticipate unpredictability and panic. Consequently, he will be engaged in defensive thought for extended periods. This, in turn, will result in the falsification of experience through the shutting out of stimuli, and will prevent him from achieving his preferences and improving his ability to predict. This seems to explain, in part, the plight of the mentally disturbed person.

It is possible to establish a crude continuum of the degree of a person's stability, ranging from adjustment to insanity, using defensiveness as the index. The well-adjusted individual does not customarily indulge in defensiveness; instead, he effectively seeks to expand his scope of prediction and pursues his preferences. The mentally disturbed individual engages in defensiveness to a substantial extent, but he is more involved in preventive defensiveness than in restorative defensiveness. He tends to shut out stimulation, thereby restricting his ability to predict, but he does not totally shut out external stimulation. The individual who drifts into episodes of insanity engages in restorative defensiveness. During these episodes he is out of touch with the environment. He shuts out the environment and becomes preoccupied with his internal feelings of panic in an effort to relieve his panic autistically so that he will be able to deal with the environment again.

The three phases described above may be compared to the lens opening of a camera. In the well-adjusted individual, the lens opening is wide open, and stimulation is selectively admitted. In the mentally disturbed individual, the lens opening is partially open, and input is restricted and biased. In the insane person, the lens opening is closed, and external stimulation is shut out for the most part during his episodes of insanity.

These explanations of insanity and mental disturbance are by no means comprehensive or conclusive, but they do suggest another approach to Freudian explanations of mental adjustment.

Individual Adjustment

Freud indicates that a neurotic is an individual who does not receive appetitive gratifications. He also suggests that neurosis and psychosis lie on a continuum—that is, as neurosis becomes more severe, it leads to psychosis. This would imply that as the individual is deprived of appetitive gratification, he moves closer to psychosis.

I am suggesting that a psychotic is what I have described as an insane individual who engages in autism to reduce panic and stabilize his mental process because he cannot maintain a predictable relationship with the environment; regardless of whether he receives appetitive gratification or not, he is in a state of fantasy in an attempt to restore his ability to predict. The reinstatement of his ability to predict would restore his sanity, not the provision of appetitive gratification. I question whether one who does not receive appetitive gratification is mentally ill solely because of his deprivation. A neurotic may be unhappy, but can deprivation of id satisfaction alone be the cause of mental illness? It would seem to make more sense to say that a person who is unable to predict appetitive gratification may be to some extent mentally ill. According to my theory, the individual's inability to predict appetitive gratification or anything else is a sign of mental illness. The inability to predict appetitive gratification is merely an important example of his general limitation.

It is always difficult and risky to superimpose one theoretical context upon another as I have done in comparing my proposed theory with Freudian theory. The comparison was intended only to explain my view of mental adjustment. I realize that these limited references to Freudian theory do not do justice to it; they simply serve to make my point. According to Freudian theory, it is the effect of id deprivation on the ego that leads to mental illness, not id deprivation alone. It should be noted, however, that Freudian theory focuses on and explains irrational behavior. My interest is in the explanation of rational behavior.

13

LEARNING

Learning is represented by the formation of memories and abstractions and the ideas they produce. The individual is motivated to learn because of the implications that learning has for predictions. Thus, because the individual is motivated to predict, and the learning of relationships is the basis for prediction, the individual is endowed with a natural tendency to learn. Formal education may occasionally thwart the natural tendency to learn if the instruction fails to demonstrate the relationship between learning and prediction.

I have described the learning process as the formation of thought proceeding on consecutive levels—from memories, to abstractions, and then to higher-level abstractions, each successive level of learning being an expansion of the preceding level. Abstractions are formed from memories, and higher-level abstractions are formed from lower-level abstractions, as learning proceeds from the specific to the general.

Because a totally unfamiliar event must be memorized to be recognized and predicted, initial learning must involve the formation of memories. Memorization of an event requires exposure to the event, accompanied by enough arousal to activate the individual's interest in learning about the event. Because exposure to an event is necessary in order for memorization to succeed, memorization of events proceeds gradually.

The individual's memories become more complex as simple events are associated into more complex events and the memories that form cover more comprehensive experiences. As this occurs, the individual is able to memorize time as well as space relationships and to note the transition from one event to another. Complex memories depict the transition of events from one state to another, and the individual is then able to predict a future state from a current state.

It was said that memorization occurs to permit an unfamiliar event to be predicted. Memorization begins because arousal has been induced when an event cannot be identified and so cannot be predicted. If an event is recognized but cannot be predicted, memorization may be initiated so that more may be learned about the event in the hope that it may become predictable.

An infant is born with no actual memories, and his early learning consists primarily of memorization of the events he experiences. Such early learning takes place gradually, in small, graded increments, as the infant is repeatedly exposed to events and gradually memorizes them. As a greater number of memories are formed into complex networks, the child becomes capable of identifying and predicting more and more events.

As memories are categorized into abstractions according to their similarities and differences, identification of an unfamiliar event can occur. The familiar features of an unfamiliar event are matched with an abstraction, and the individual recognizes that the features belong to a group of similar things. He is then able to conclude that the predictions that can be made about the abstraction can also be made about the unfamiliar event in question. In this way he learns to identify and predict unfamiliar events.

As the individual's inventory of abstractions increases, he is able to recognize and predict a greater number of unfamiliar events through the deliberation of abstractions. Moreover, because fewer events will be totally unfamiliar to him, he will encounter fewer occasions for memorization.

Identification and prediction of unfamiliar events by deliberating abstractions occurs relatively promptly through insight, as compared with the alternative process of memorization. As the individual matures and more memories form, a greater number of

Some Implications of the Theory

his experiences will be familiar. As more abstractions form, he will be able to recognize more often familiar features of unfamiliar events. The more memories and abstractions that are formed, the greater the number of events that can be predicted.

Since abstractions provide the basis for making choices, a person's potential for selecting programs and goals by comparison increases substantially as he matures and becomes more capable of forming more abstractions. This makes deliberation a more productive means of predicting and tends to increase the frequency with which the individual uses deliberation in preference to automatic matching in the quest for prediction. Furthermore, as the individual matures and resorts to deliberation more often, his behavior will become more flexible and less automatic or stereotyped.

He will also be able to make more predictions concerning unfamiliar as well as familiar events as he learns to reorganize and refine abstractions. Although abstractions are formed from memories, these abstractions may be reorganized and refined through experience (and directed educational procedures) in such a way as to allow the memories themselves to be reorganized on the basis of other criteria. A single memory can then be classified into several (perhaps hundreds of) categories or abstractions (for example, the *red ball* that *bounces* is *mine*). These memories and abstractions serve in the derivation and testing of predictions in the learning process.

Predictions are derived from neuroprints which portray transitions from events that are happening to events that may happen. When a match for identification occurs, the individual is to some extent aware of what is happening. Subsequently, during the match for prediction, a neuroprint is elicited that portrays a transition from the event that is happening at that moment to an event that may be expected to happen in the future. From a master neuroprint the individual is then able to deduce, not only the prediction of what may happen in the future, but also a program that can be predicted to lead to the future happening.

Predictions deduced from memories prompt the individual to predict that future events will happen in the same way that he has experienced them before; he will expect repetition of familiar events. But abstractions permit the unfamiliar to be predicted, thus providing the basis for discovery and allowing the individual to expect novel experiences.

The comparison between memories and abstractions suggests two different modes of learning a prediction. A prediction may be learned by memorizing both the initiating event and the outcome to which it may lead; the outcome is then predicted solely on the basis of memory. Or a prediction may be learned through abstraction, in which case the prediction is deduced by insight. Learning to predict from abstractions through insight depends upon the existence of the memories and abstractions needed, plus the ability of the individual to deliberate them to generate the prediction.

Once predictions are derived from a master neuroprint, they are tested by matching the program portion of the master neuroprint with ensuing events to determine whether it leads toward the goal as predicted. The program directs the actions of the individual as he proceeds toward the goal by executing and testing each progressive subroutine of the program. Because the individual strives to confirm his predictions, he will adjust his actions or the program to obtain a match between the neuroprints in his mind and the events.

In chapter 5 it was stated that the individual has gained control over his environment when a program he elicits prescribes actions that are predicted to lead to a goal and actually do lead to that goal. He has learned how to take action to achieve the goal in the future. Such prediction and control have important implications for learning.

Control implies prediction. If an event can be controlled, it can also be predicted. For instance, if an individual can obtain food whenever he wants it, he has control over its acquisition. He is then able to predict that when he wants food he can obtain it. But it is also possible for a person to be able to predict an event without being able to control it. Hurricanes can be predicted but cannot be controlled to any great extent as yet. Although the ability to predict an event does not imply the ability to control

SOME IMPLICATIONS OF THE THEORY

the event, it often implies the ability to control one's actions in relation to the event. In the preceding example, although the hurricane itself cannot be controlled, the individual, upon predicting that one is imminent, may seek refuge in a storm cellar to avoid the hurricane. In other words, when the individual learns how to control an event, he also learns how to predict it. However, when he learns how to predict the event he does not necessarily learn how to control it but may learn how to control his relationship to it, either seeking or avoiding it as he chooses.

According to this theory, the individual is likely to seek to extend his ability to predict and control events as much as he is able, to gain from them whatever benefits they might provide for him. If he fails to dominate an event in this fashion, he will seek to control his own actions to avoid an encounter with that event, so that he need not feel threatened by it. Consequently, even though he is not able to manipulate the event as he chooses, it will still be predictable and he can adjust his actions to avoid it if that is to his advantage. Finally, if he fails both to manipulate the event and to avoid it, he will tend to think about the event in an effort to conceive ideas that will make it predictable. Man's desire to predict and control himself in his environment tends to lead him to an increasing mastery of his relationship with the environment.

When an event is unpredictable, the individual will repeatedly attempt to predict it, especially if excessive arousal is associated with the event.[1] Moreover, once he is confident that he has conceived of a program that will enable him to predict how to control a disturbing or painful event, he will seek to encounter it again so as to test his prediction. As I have said earlier, in this sense and under these conditions people seek painful experiences.

Environmental feedback also affects prediction. Because it is common to think of environmental effects on learning in terms of punishment and reward, I shall use these terms in the following discussion. When predictions are validated, it may be said

---

[1] This is an interpretation of Freud's "repetition compulsion" within the framework of my theory.

that the individual has been rewarded by his encounter with the environment because his desire to predict is fulfilled when the program that he predicts will lead to a prescribed goal is confirmed by environmental feedback. His desire to predict would not be rewarded if he achieved the goal by accident, because he would not have learned anything that would enable him to predict how to achieve the goal in the future and thus gain control over his environment. If the program directing his actions does not lead to the goal as predicted, the experience may be regarded as either challenging or punishing. An environmental encounter may be regarded as challenging if the individual learns from the experience what program modifications are necessary to lead to the goal in the future. The original program is not totally invalidated but, rather, delimited and refined. It is like finding out what not to do, while learning what to do, in order to achieve a goal. Although the individual's attempt to confirm his predictions has been thwarted at the moment, learning has taken place that makes it possible for him to try again with some hope for success.

An environmental experience may be considered punishing if a program predicted to lead to a goal is not confirmed and feedback gives no indication of how to modify the program to achieve the goal. Under these circumstances, the individual does not learn what to do and so cannot modify his behavior to pursue the goal with any hope for success in the future. The encounter may be regarded as punishing because it is a confirmation of the individual's inability to predict.

Although punishment has long been used as a means of teaching children to conform, psychologists and educators have been aware of its limitations. Perhaps the foregoing interpretation may help to explain why punishment is an ineffective means for promoting learning. If, through punishment, the individual merely learns what not to do but gains no insight into what he might do to achieve success, then punishment cannot promote success. The individual learns only that the punished alternative does not prove successful. Limitless possibilities still remain to be tried by him, but the experience gives him no indication of how to proceed. In addition, it should be noted that a main effect of punishment is its interference with the execution of motor programs. The individual learns not to put programs into action to test their predictions because of the punishment he anticipates.

Thorndike noted as early as 1932 that punishment left much to be desired as a method of influencing behavior. The results of comparisons with other methods all tell the same story. Rewarding a connection always strengthened it substantially; punishing it weakened it little or not at all. Hilgard, commenting on some of Thorndike's experiments, reported that a number of experiments yielded data showing that the effects of reward and punishment were not equal and opposite, as had been implied in earlier statements of the effects of satisfiers and of annoyers. Instead, under conditions in which symmetrical action was possible, reward appeared to be much more powerful than punishment. This conclusion, if confirmed, can be of immense social importance in such fields of application as education and criminology.

In discussing Skinner's work on the relationship between reward and punishment, Hilgard concluded that, according to Skinner and his followers, punishment is defined as an experimental arrangement whose effects remain to be investigated empirically. The *arrangement* is the opposite of reinforcement (although the *effects* are not opposite), so that two main cases arise: (1) the presentation of a negative reinforcer, and (2) the removal of a positive reinforcer. If at the beginning of extinction the rat is slapped on its feet when it presses the lever, its rate of responding is depressed, but it eventually recovers. The total responses to extinction have not been reduced by the punishment, as they should be if the punishment were negative conditioning. There is here some support for Thorndike's belief that punishments do not act opposite to rewards.[2]

More will be said about reinforcement in chapter 15, when I shall discuss the opportunity to predict and control.

Even when a prediction is confirmed, there will be some discrepancy between the prescription of the program that led to the

[2] Ernest R. Hilgard, *Theories of Learning*, 2nd ed., pp. 113–14.

goal and the actual events that occurred, because no existing situation will conform exactly to any program. Programs are developed from past experience, and the present is always somewhat different than the past. The discrepancies between the program being tested and events reveal novel stimuli that are at that moment unpredictable. The novel stimuli provide the occasion on which the learning process may be initiated again—that is, they represent a specific event that may be matched for identification and prediction with memories and abstractions. During the process the predictions of the novel stimuli are derived and then tested.

There is still another factor that contributes to learning and prediction: public resources for learning. One of the advantages of being a human being is that each of us can profit from the store of knowledge recorded by our forefathers. Not only is information available, but also society has provided for the transmission of information through its educational establishments. In short, an increasing wealth of ideas is passed on systematically from one generation to the next.

In the early stages of development, the young child is provided with pictures of relationships among the events he can be expected to encounter as he matures. They are first presented to him as "still pictures" in the pages of a book because this stable presentation of the composition of objects may help him to recognize them. Although the still picture may imply action and transition, the child's instructor will usually point to one object at a time, naming it for him and then asking him to name it.

In the early stages, learning of the content of these still pictures corresponds to the learning of nouns in language. Then transitions are noted for the child so that he may learn time as well as space relationships. This enables him to understand events and to make predictions about the events he recognizes. Observation of live actions in the panorama of life enhances prediction. In language, this understanding includes transitive verbs, which become associated with nouns to express the understanding of time relationships. As the child's instructor names objects, he often refers

—unwittingly, perhaps—to the category or abstraction to which the object belongs. Upon seeing a robin, the instructor may call it a bird, and the child will learn the names of abstractions at least as often as he learns the specific names of objects.

In the course of his formal education, the child may learn a set of related abstractions in the form of a taxonomy. For instance, he may be taught the phylogenetic scale, which is a taxonomy that classifies living things. It is composed of levels of abstractions, each of which describes a type of living creature—for example, fish, amphibians, reptiles, birds, mammals, and so forth. The scale was devised by Darwin and others through the observation and classification of all living things. Another example of a public abstraction is the periodic table, which classifies the elements. It was formed through the observation and classification of minerals.

These elaborate taxonomic systems represent man's current knowledge of the similarities and differences among events. What many children could learn about taxonomies but do not is that, because abstractions permit predictions to be made about novel events, they can be used to discover things that may advance the knowledge not only of the naïve individual but of mankind as well. The taxonomy, which represents what man knows about a class of events, may be used to deduce what man may still discover about the class of events. Since a taxonomy is an abstraction, it portrays relationships, and, as I have said, it is the knowledge of relationships that allows predictions to be made.

The item to be discovered may be defined as a gap, blank space, or missing part of the taxonomy. The characteristics of the missing part can be deduced from its relative position in the taxonomy —that is, it will be more like the things adjacent to it in the taxonomy and less like the things farther removed from it. It can therefore be predicted that an entity can be found with these specific characteristics. The missing part of the taxonomy can then be sought.

For example, not too long ago, it was determined that there were missing parts of the phylogenetic scale in the category "mammals." It was deduced that mammals existed at one time that fit into the scale between apes and humans, with certain characteristics that would place them in that position. This deduction generated the prediction that fossil remains of mammals with such characteristics could be found. Such "missing links" were subsequently found, although their identification is by no means a settled matter. These deductions were made by recognizing missing parts of abstractions and deducing their characteristics by conceptualizing the relationship between the parts and the whole of the categorical arrangements.

The known facts about the periodic table were used in a similar way to discover new elements. When the table was completed initially, it showed the relationships of all the elements that were known at the time. But there were blank spaces in the table to indicate the probable existence of elements yet to be discovered. The position of a blank space in the taxonomy defined the characteristics of the elements to be discovered in much the same way as the characteristics of the "missing links" were defined by their position in the phylogenetic scale. On the basis of the information in the taxonomy, new elements were sought and discovered.

Abstractions provide a singular potential for discovery because they permit the learner to deduce unknown events and to understand their characteristics. The learner can then conceive of a program to search for the unknown, with the possibility of discovering it. To take the example cited earlier, when the characteristics of the "missing links" were deduced, a program could be conceived to search for the fossil remains of such mammals in a probable location; the deduction not only specified the characteristics of the mammals but also suggested where and how the remains might be found.

The abstractions in the mind of the individual learner represent what he himself knows about the relationship among events, and the discoveries generated by his abstractions will be new to him. If the learner is all mankind, the abstractions represent what all men know about a class of events, and the discoveries deduced from these abstractions, if confirmed, will be new to all mankind.

Probably the most important function of society is the transmittal of knowledge to the individual concerning programs for processing information to conceive predictions and programs for testing predictions. So-called facts are available in libraries but, with accelerated change, facts now become obsolete faster than ever before. Moreover, the vast number of facts that have accumulated in man's store of knowledge is more than any student is able to absorb and retain, even when he eventually specializes in some subject area. Programs that prescribe methods of obtaining facts and for generating and testing predictions based on these facts provide a much more effective, stable, and limited base of knowledge for problem solving. A student who learns how to acquire and use information can stay abreast of the times, whereas a student who studies facts is often led to the false belief that what he may need to know in the future is already available to him as fact in the existing reservoir of knowledge.

Society provides information on programs that can be used to formulate and test predictions. These programs may be found in the field of logic, where inductive and deductive reasoning may be learned. However, few students nowadays study formal logic, and those who do are generally not taught the relationships between logic and the formulation and testing of predictions. In deductive logic, for example, the student is taught that the product of deduction is a conclusion. I maintain that what should be regarded as the product of deduction is a prediction that is logically valid but one that must be tested against subsequent events in order to determine its experiential or empirical validity.

In the previous two chapters, I focused on the individual to consider some direct implications of the theory. I now move to consider some important, but less direct, implications.

14

Systematic Prediction and Control

Society's contribution to the development of the individual's thought and behavior consists in providing the environmental conditions that affect his ability to predict.

We have seen how the individual predicts and controls himself in the environment in accordance with his subjective preferences. Subjective judgments, however, tend to be influenced strongly by the emotional components of thought. As a result, the individual's thought and behavior are often idiosyncratic and understandable to himself alone. Such thought and behavior represents his personalized style. They need no justification other than his assertion that he thinks and acts as he does because he prefers to behave that way.

On the other hand, when the individual is involved in pursuing a predetermined outcome, he becomes more interested in the probabilities of achieving success through various courses of action and the cost of proceeding toward the outcome in the various ways. In other words, he becomes content-oriented and tends to focus on the substantive aspects of the problem at hand rather than on his immediate personal feelings. A typical instance of such an approach is an individual's attitude during the work week. He concentrates on achieving an outcome, rather than on the way he feels about the events of the moment. Most probably he is working with a group to produce something the group considers to be of benefit. To some extent, he sets aside his personal preferences during working hours to meet the demands of the group. Then on payday he may use the money he receives to pursue his own preferences.

The content of thought provides the basis for a great deal more objectivity than does the emotion associated with thought. Substantive problems—such as the probabilities, means, and costs of achieving an outcome—are often solved with the assistance of some objective systems provided by society (e.g., statistics and cost analysis). These systems are available for the individual to learn, whether he is working on a problem by himself or with a group, and the procedures for operating them are objective. They may be used by anyone who has learned the appropriate procedures, and the procedures are the same for everyone.

Although each individual follows any given set of procedures in his own personalized style (e.g., driving a car), his ability to vary from the prescribed method of operation is usually quite limited. But the content of his thoughts, during his leisure, may be recruited to satisfy his emotions. Then the choices he makes are a matter of personal taste. They are more private than public.

Let us now move to a discussion of systematic prediction and control, which will primarily concern work-oriented thought and action based upon the content of experience.

The individual's ambitions to predict and control are fulfilled through an objective, a systematic, and a scientific approach to problems. It is the aim of science as well as of the individual to improve prediction and control, so it is not surprising that science has received such general endorsement.

Systematic prediction and control involves the use of various types of systems. A system is a set of relationships that is publicly identifiable; the set of relationships is objective in the sense that people can agree upon its organization. Because of this, one event within the system can be predicted from another, and the individual who learns the system can use it to make predictions.

The term *system* is obviously a very broad one, and examples of systems are numerous. For our purposes, four kinds of systems

SYSTEMATIC PREDICTION AND CONTROL

need to be distinguished: natural physical systems, social systems, a combination of these two, and problem-solving systems.

A natural physical system is a phenomenon of nature that functions without the assistance of man and includes the relationships of physical substance. One example of such a system is the rain cycle, which includes bodies of water such as lakes and rivers, clouds and rain. Other examples of natural physical systems are seasonal changes and the effects of the moon on the tide.

Social systems are created by man through social agreement. They have no physical substance. They are, in essence, thought systems. They exist and have force because men have agreed that they shall exist and have force. The monetary system is a social system. Money exists by virtue of social agreement and has force because men have agreed it shall have force—that is, purchasing power. Legal systems and language are other examples of social systems. Social systems are conveyed by means of physical substance simply to make them tangible—for example, money takes the form of metal coin and paper—but the systems themselves have no physical substance.

The automobile and other machines are illustrations of the combination of social and physical systems. Machines are created by man, but the physical substances of which they are composed are integral parts of the actual functioning of the system. In a pure social system, the physical matter is not a functional component of the system. For instance, in a legal system, the paper on which laws are written is not needed each time the laws are enforced. On the other hand, the operation of the automobile depends upon an ordered operation of the physical parts of the car.

A problem-solving system is a system of ordered relationships used to predict and control. It is obvious from what has been said that all systems can be used to predict, even natural systems. There is only one general prerequisite to enable one to predict—learning the relationships of the system. However, the relationships within the system must be stable. In order for the individual to use the system for purposes of control, he must not only learn the system, he must also be able to manipulate some of the relationships of the system. Thus, the ordering of events within the system promotes prediction, and the ability to manipulate components of the system promotes control.

Artificial systems—that is, systems created by man for man—are created to be manipulated by man. They are created to increase not only his predictive ability but his control of his environment as well. Many natural systems, such as hurricanes, can be predicted but not controlled by man. Social systems and sociophysical systems like machines can be used for both prediction and control. Knowing the value of money enables one to predict that he needs money to subsist. When he has it, he can control what he buys. When one understands an automobile, he can predict that if he turns the ignition key the engine will start. He can then turn the key to control the starting of the engine.

Mathematics is a pure social system that can be used for both prediction and control. It can be used to measure and compare quantities of any phenomena that are measurable. There are various types of mathematical systems, among them geometry, algebra, and bookkeeping.

Systems exist independently of man and are also created by him. For greater control over these systems, man duplicates them, as it were, via symbolic representations. Words and other symbols come to stand for objects and relationships in reality. "Models" of reality, both physical and abstract, serve to assist man in his manipulation of reality, and even in his understanding of it. Man uses and develops problem-solving systems.

As a social being, man quickly acquires language, and this opens the door for him to all the abstract systems that surround him in his home and, later, in the outside world. This process begins, in fact, during his childhood, in his complex interaction with his parents—especially the mother—in the acquisition of language symbols. The development of language in the child involves the evolution of vocal expression from random sounds into selectively reinforced ones, by which the child acquires vocal control over small segments of his environment, along with some degree of imitation of adult speech patterns, which likewise leads to control. As soon as there is some common bond of socially established linguistic agreement between child and parent, the child learns not only from his own successes in establishing control (e.g., first by crying and later by asking for things) but also from instruction by the parents, who begin to feed life-preservative systems to him (e.g., warnings about hot objects and, later, about traffic). Most of this is done by using language.

A distinction should be made here between language and problem-solving systems. Language itself solves only one problem— that of communication. Once communication exists, something more specific is always involved in the content of a problem-solving system. Language is merely the matrix of these more specific symbolic systems. (Since language can be used to give both misinformation and bad advice, it is, in fact, capable of impeding the solution of a problem.)

Once the child has learned the communication system to some degree, he has the problem of fitting previously learned concepts into the symbolic language of his society. With language, of course, he has acquired greater control, since he can now initiate effective control. As his inventory of ideas grows, his potential for prediction and control quickly increases, because he is now able to make his wishes known and to enlist other people (usually adults) in gratifying these wishes. Language probably also assists him by enabling him to identify and keep in mind even fleeting desires. Thus, in the absence of the candy he may want, he can repeat the word *candy* persistently, fixing the idea in his mind and keeping it alive despite the distraction of later stimuli.

With his language now established—and, through it, access to the symbolic systems of his family and of his environment attained—the child is ready to incorporate into his individual thought the systems of his elders. At first, of course, this is not a matter of his choice. His parents are anxious to teach him systems that are socially acceptable. For instance, the system he will be taught with regard to elimination may be initially repulsive to him, but it will turn out to be a neater and more satisfactory solution to his problems in this area, with less discomfort, than his previous solutions were. Besides learning such systems as this and others (e.g., improved methods of eating), the child also acquires systems more congenial to him. He welcomes the learning of methods to keep warm in cold weather (such as wrapping a scarf around his neck), and of making toys operate interestingly by turning handles that wind them up, and of making structures by putting blocks one on top of another, and of making a bigger object by fitting one object into another.

Problem-solving systems aid in arriving at predictions, establishing a plan of action to fulfill the predictions, and devising methods of evaluating progress toward the intended outcome. A problem-solving system may be used to produce a desired state of thought as well as a desired state of being. Thought can be improved inductively by learning new relationships or deductively by establishing new and accurate predictions. A desired state of being may be produced (e.g., acquisition of a physical object) by establishing a plan of action (e.g., procedures for negotiating with the environment to produce the item desired) to fulfill one's intention.

Each problem-solving system includes elements that are related —as are x and y in algebra, and brick and mortar in the construction of a building. The relationship between the elements must be defined so that the system may be used to solve particular problems. Problem solving involves predicting from the ordered relationship of elements within a system and manipulating these components to achieve a desired outcome.

This does not mean, however, that all inferences must be made by making quantitative comparisons. Perhaps all inferences can be made in that way, but in many instances this procedure would be a waste of time and effort. This is particularly true with respect to decision making. A person makes decisions by considering previously learned relationships. Most of his conclusions are the result of rather simple, primitive comparisons. He may not even be aware of the relationships he is using to draw his inferences.

It becomes clear, then, that the individual can predict and control more efficiently and accurately if he utilizes the systems provided him by his society. If he learns the systems and learns when and how to use them, he will have, in the combination of ideas and systems, more potent tools for problem solving than are ideas alone. For example, ideas alone can be used to estimate—either by the naked eye or with the assistance of a rope—the length of an object, but this method is neither as efficient nor as accurate as using the metric system to measure length. Or the individual can keep track of time by observing the passage of days, moons, and seasons, but these methods are not as precise or as efficient as using a watch or a calendar.

The use of tools—such as pliers, hammers, and saws—and machines—such as autos, stoves, and refrigerators—also multiplies man's effectiveness enormously. The utilization of each tool and machine requires great expenditure of thought for its manufacture, repair, and maintenance. However, the benefits that accrue to man in their utilization far outweigh the investment he makes in manufacturing them and in tolerating some of their deleterious side effects. Although each tool and machine has a special purpose, it is used to complement or substitute for man's personal effort. Pliers and steam shovels complement man's muscles. Servomechanisms such as the thermostat complement man's nervous system by reacting to what would be man's stimulus input and responding for him (e.g., a thermostat reacts to changes in temperature and responds by turning the heating or cooling system on and off). The computer complements even higher functions of man; it is capable of solving mathematical problems more rapidly and more accurately than man can. In short, prediction and control are facilitated when systems are used to complement thought and action.

Once an individual has learned how to employ problem-solving systems, his actions can be better understood if the goal he intends to pursue and the program he intends to employ to achieve it are known. In attempting to understand behavior, we often draw inferences from a person's actions alone. This seriously limits the predictions that can be inferred from our observations, because the predictions are necessarily of a relatively molecular and short-term nature.

The drafting of blueprints for the establishment of social goals and programs has more importance than may be realized from a

162

casual glance. Congressional appropriations are made to achieve goals, and the guidelines that specify how government funds shall be spent represent plans formulated to achieve these goals.

An example of the importance of social goals and plans is a recent victory over the lamprey eel. A few years ago the sea lamprey invaded the Great Lakes, attacking and killing lake trout. The problem became so serious that some feared that the lake trout might become extinct. Then public sentiment brought action. Money was appropriated to study ways of controlling the sea lamprey. Eventually a chemical was discovered that killed the lamprey in its spawning ground, and the lake trout were saved.

The sea lamprey's initial conquest of the lake trout followed the law of natural selection. This law governs events in the environment without regard for man's interventions. Man's defeat of the sea lamprey is an example of social selection, based upon social intention and implemented according to a plan. This, of course, reflects man's shaping the elements of his environment to his preferences.

The importance of social selection should not be underrated. One's social group influences the determination of the problems selected to be solved; the individuals selected to work on a problem; the selection of systems to be used in solving it (e.g., the method used to teach a course); permissible solutions (it is not permissible to deprive children of food in order to improve their learning); the information that can be used to solve it (censorship affects the availability of information); the ways in which that information can be used (information classified as "top secret" can be used only under certain limited conditions); what shall be taught (e.g., democracy rather than communism); how information shall be regarded (in the United States, both the teacher and the learner are expected to value democracy above communism); and what systems shall be invented or improved (current social bias favors the invention and improvement of systems that can be used to conquer cancer).

Let us consider the effects such social selection has on the individual. Social values generate emotional reactions to experiences and, consequently, to thought, thereby creating an impulse toward or against certain thoughts and types of behavior. When society endorses certain thoughts and types of behavior, the individual tends to think and act in the prescribed way. Social sanctions generate motivation to seek or avoid certain experiences. Social prohibitions then create and institutionalize defensiveness, especially in the very young. This in turn can limit the accuracy and availability of the information an individual is able to bring to bear on a given problem. If internalization of a social pattern involves anything that inhibits thought, prediction is damaged. If certain types of thoughts are regarded as taboo, the individual in whom this value is internalized will conform and not think those thoughts.

I maintain that the individual can be taught to predict the consequences of his actions. He can learn the differences between thought consequences and action consequences. He can learn that the only consequence of thought is action and that it is action that brings response from the environment, including sanctions from one's social group. With this perspective, the individual can learn to deliberate the consequences of alternative courses of action without trepidation and to select one to follow, with an expectation of what will happen as a result. Because he makes a volitional choice, he has reason to accept the consequences of his actions.

On the other hand, if the individual learns that the consideration of certain alternatives is forbidden, he tends not to learn the consequences of these alternatives. He may, for instance, learn to regard certain actions—and even thoughts about these actions—as "sinful." But the consequences of sin are too often mysterious and cannot be validated; such consequences are often promised in the hereafter. The individual lives in fear of a retaliation it is impossible for him to identify or predict. Thought, action, and consequences, then, become unrelated empirically.

Prediction and control culminate in the individual when he is able to consider the consequences of alternative actions and selects the course of action he prefers. This includes deliberating the empirical consequences of violating or conforming to social expectations and deciding whether he wishes to conform or not.

Some Implications of the Theory

From the perspective of society, nearly all influences on the individual—many of them generated indirectly via social institutions and culture—either foster or retard the development of his ability to predict. Since it is, in fact, both in his interest and in that of society for him to attain such capabilities, the general implication for public policy seems clear: every major social taboo against thought should be discarded, because by restricting the individual's ability to predict, it reduces his effectiveness as a social being.

I shall close the chapter in a speculative fashion by comparing the attitudes of children and adults on certain social issues. Children are known to be less "inhibited" than adults—that is, they engage in types of behavior that adults avoid. Behavior that is negativistic, highly emotional, obviously selfish, impolite, and so forth, is in violation of the social code to which adults have learned to subscribe. On occasion, of course, such behavior may be seen in adults, when induced by conditions of stress, long deprivation, and the like. In common parlance, adults "know better" than to behave in this way, although the impulse to do so must certainly persist. Social approval or disapproval is a key factor in determining their behavior. (Other social influences on thought and action will be discussed later.) Among the adult's ideas are many that inform him in advance (enabling prediction) concerning the reactions of others to his behavior. To the extent that other people are crucial to his purposes, the adult does not want to incur their opposition. Hence, he moderates his behavior to some standard that will enlist their toleration, support, and friendship. Furthermore, since the issues involved in social conformity are typically rather petty and detailed (having to do with such matters as keeping one's shoes shined, one's buttons buttoned, and so forth), much of this conformity is simply relegated to habit. When the child fails to observe these rituals, he is not displaying uninhibitedness, but ignorance. He has not yet developed the fine mesh of habits in which the adult envelops himself. Thus far, the distinction favors the adult, who is not having to go through the pain of learning anew thousands of little habits, having them, instead, already in his repertory.

Systematic Prediction and Control

Beyond a certain point, however, the balance changes somewhat. The adult becomes, to some extent, a prisoner of his own habits, and begins to seek conformity for its own sake. Especially in highly mannered, ritualized, and formalized societies, the adult may lose sight of his own purposes in his zeal for social acceptance. The charm of childhood seems to increase in the eyes of such adults, who wistfully observe the child's freedom from the pressures of ritual. This so-called freedom, of course, is only relative to the absurd situation of the adult—and what is more, the child in such a society, under ever-increasing pressure to learn the many ins and outs of his social group, does not at all feel that he has the amount of freedom attributed to him by his elders, who are, in fact, quite busily depriving him of it as fast as they can.

In a very complex society, where there is formal social pressure but no single standard of conformity and many options exist for the individual, some adults may become overinhibited. It is the contrast between such compulsive, highly conformist, and fear-ridden adults and children in general that partially justifies the notion that children are freer.

In addition, in a complex adult society, the demands of society may become so exacting that all individuals become rigid, to some extent, in areas they do not have time to deliberate about. A great deal of mislearning may then occur, as the individual is likely to take much on ill-considered faith from others and consign it to habit. These are the areas in which the child's "insight" may suddenly appear profound, but the truth is that he simply does not yet know enough to be wrong. Given time and further instruction, he will be as wrong as anyone else. This is perhaps especially apparent in children's instinctive reactions to other people. The behavior of adults toward each other may become so reflexive as to preclude serious consideration of each other's qualities. The child, however, tends to look at the facts without prejudice and to make more-just judgments—hence such expressions as "out of the mouths of babes." In our lamentable lack of interest in people as individuals, the child's insight may appear profound. The same is true, to a lesser degree, of the four-year-old's "profound" philosophical question "Daddy, why is God?"

or the nine-year-old's more subtle "Is wise deeper than clever?" The adult may long ago have stopped thinking about the first; the distinction in the second may have long since joined his repertory of reflexive assertions in dealing with the semantic distinctions of his own language. Yet only an adult, with his fully developed reason, can best appreciate and ponder these questions on issues he may have disposed of when he was much less capable mentally.

Conformity that restricts thought is harmful because it inhibits prediction. However, when the individual conforms to rules and standards in order to learn the taxonomies, programs, and systems society provides to facilitate prediction, conformity may, indeed, be beneficial.

15

The Opportunity to Predict and Control

In the formal theory presented in this book, I have posited prediction as a basic motive impelling human behavior and have described mental operations as functioning to fulfill this motive. As we have seen, some environmental arrangements tend to promote prediction while others seem to thwart it. In my judgment, it is necessary to provide environmental conditions that promote prediction in any type of behavior modification, such as conditioning, education, or therapy. The following speculations about the way in which the environment should be arranged to facilitate prediction may be suggested by my theory as to how predictions are conceived and confirmed. However, the validity of that theory does not rest upon the validity of these speculations. I wish to consider whether the environment can be arranged in one way or another to facilitate prediction. If it can be, the promotion of prediction can be purposeful and helpful, especially for teachers, who can use it as a key to the understanding of human behavior and as a tool to encourage learning.

As I have stated in chapter 13, there are three ways in which environmental feedback can affect the testing of a prediction: by validating it, by refuting it, or by cuing the correct way of validating it. An encounter that results in validation will be rewarding, while one that results in refutation will be regarded as punishment, because it shows the error of the individual's action without indicating the correct action. When feedback does suggest the right action, the encounter will be regarded as challenging, though initially somewhat thwarting.

When a prediction is refuted by feedback it can cause defensiveness. The environment is regarded as unpredictable, and the punishment it provides can cause the individual to shut out what seems to him to be alien surroundings. Because punishment can cause defensiveness, which in turn can impair prediction (as I have explained in chapter 11), punitive experiences are to be avoided.

This position on punishment is generally supported in the literature that deals with reinforcement. One of the best-known of these studies is the article by Estes published in 1944, in which he concludes that punishment is not generally useful because, among other reasons, it also suppresses responses other than the one at which the punishment is directed.[1] I would explain this phenomenon by suggesting that a person may become defensive when his predictions are not validated, particularly if he already lacks self-confidence.

To best promote prediction, the environment should be arranged so that it will provide the opportunity for an individual's predictions to be confirmed and will simultaneously provide feedback to cue the correct response if his initial attempt should fail (since there can be no guarantee that an individual will be able to confirm his prediction on any given attempt, nor is that always a desirable outcome). That kind of an environment will be regarded as rewarding or challenging but never punitive, and the individual in it will be able to expand his scope of prediction. In other words, the environment should be so arranged that as an individual attempts to confirm a prediction, a match may occur between the neuroprints in his mind and the events. If this is not possible, the feedback should provide cues so as to obtain a match.

The arrangement must, of course, take into account the predictions that the individual's ideas can support; otherwise, he will

[1] William K. Estes, "An Experimental Study of Punishment."

have no opportunity to formulate or test his predictions. His inventory of ideas must contain ideas that will permit a prediction to be confirmed on an initial attempt as well as ideas that will permit modifications to be made in his original program so that he may confirm his prediction on a subsequent attempt should his first attempt fail. Both the mind and the environment must be ready in order for a prediction to be confirmed.

Let us consider an example that illustrates mental and environmental readiness to confirm a prediction. Suppose a child is asked to cut a piece of paper to fit an outline of a square on a blackboard. To confirm his predictions on an initial attempt, the child would need to understand the idea of the shape of a square, to be able to execute the program necessary for cutting the square out of the piece of paper, and to fit the cutout to the outline on the board. For feedback to cue the correct response should his first attempt fail, the child would need to understand more than the shape of a square; he would also need to understand the idea of size, so that if he cut the square too large or too small, he could modify his actions to cut the square to the proper size on subsequent attempts. In order for the environment to be ready for the confirmation of the prediction, there should be a sharp pair of scissors, paper, and a blackboard with a distinct outline of a square on it. Finally, but most important, all environmental cues other than those provided specifically to encourage the confirmation of the prediction should be neutral, so that they will not distract the child from the task at hand.

From what has been said it can be seen that, to be most conducive to adaptive learning, the environmental arrangement should: (1) provide feedback that will permit an individual to confirm his predictions; (2) contain cues that will guide him to the correct program of action should a given program fail; and (3) be such that cues that do not lead to the confirmation of the prediction remain neutral or irrelevant.

Although people learn from all environmental encounters, my main concern is with the intentional arrangement of the environment to accomplish specific, predetermined outcomes or objectives —in effect, teaching. Thus, teaching is concerned with arranging the environment—both social and physical—so that certain predictions may be validated.

The relationship between thought and action is a problem we seldom come to grips with in teaching. The environment cannot be arranged in the manner I am prescribing unless the teacher is aware of the predictions the learner is capable of formulating and the ways in which he is capable of acting in testing a given prediction. If this is not known, the environment cannot be arranged so as to enable him to validate his prediction or to protect him from punishment. We are focusing here on one of the major difficulties in teaching—how to attain a knowledge of the learner's readiness to learn. From my point of view, readiness involves the learner's readiness to formulate predictions through ideation and to test them through action in an environment that will support validation.

If the learner is able to understand the ways in which his thoughts and actions will expand his ability to predict and control, he will be motivated to follow the teacher's suggestions. He must have confidence, however, that he will be able to validate his predictions. The teacher should assess the learner's readiness and try to convince him that he will succeed if he tries.

The teacher is the mediator between society and the learner. His job is to teach the individual to predict the environment. As I have said earlier, an individual who cannot predict efficiently can be of little value to himself or his society.

As a mediator between the learner and his environment, the teacher is in a position to interpret the environment for him. The teacher helps him to formulate accurate predictions and to take correct actions to validate his predictions. The learner, however, should not regard the teacher's actions as punitive or he will see the teacher as an enemy who prevents him from confirming his predictions and will defend against the teacher's influence. The teacher will then lose his effectiveness. On the other hand, if the teacher is considered to be an ally who is interested in helping the learner to predict, the teacher's influence will increase considerably. When the teacher has gained his pupil's confidence, he may persuade him to continue trying even when his predictions are not validated. The distinction between irrelevant environmental feedback and the issuing of punishment by the environment is seldom clear in the face of insecurity. When the learner believes he is being punished, the teacher may persuade him to believe that he has simply misread environmental cues. The teacher may interpret the learner's ideas and actions as irrelevant to prevailing environmental demands and suggest that anyone acting as he did would meet with frustration. The teacher may assure him that he is in no danger and guide him toward correct thought and action.

Teaching may be separated into two domains, education and therapy; the above statements apply to both kinds of teaching. Although I am not attempting to set forth theories of education and therapy, it may be possible to derive such theories from the postulates about prediction and control I have formulated. The basic principles of my theory may be applied in education and therapy because these fields are involved in changing behavior and in regulating opportunities to predict and control.

Education is essentially developmental in character. It is concerned with the learning of new predictions, which, of course, must be founded upon the capacity and readiness of the individual being taught. Adaptive learning involves the learning of new and accurate predictions. Mislearning occurs when the individual learns inaccurate predictions. Because there are nuances in all problems, even in those seemingly met with before, in order for a prediction to be most accurate, it must account for the novel in any encounter.

When mislearning occurs, it interferes with development, and relearning becomes necessary, because accurate predictions cannot be built upon inaccurate predictions. Relearning is the process of correcting inaccurate predictions. Therapy is the process of correcting inaccurate predictions so that education may be resumed effectively.

The teaching of deliberation is crucial in promoting all adaptive learning because through deliberation one learns to predict the novel. An individual learns to make accurate predictions on the ideational level by deliberating alternative solutions to a problem.

SOME IMPLICATIONS OF THE THEORY

Teaching deliberation is not a simple task. Initial learning is the learning of habits. The individual first learns one way of approaching a problem before he learns alternatives. He continues to use a habit because if an idea has worked in the past he can expect it to enable him to maintain predictability when it is applied to a current problem. This explains why the child continues to use habits instead of learning alternatives. Security comes with self-confidence, and self-confidence is built upon the validation of predictions. Moreover, the easiest predictions to validate are those that have been validated before. The repeated use of habits in early childhood is a natural, although primitive, tendency. Since habits can be used adaptively, later learning tends to be built upon early learning rather than replacing it. But excessive repetition of habits often characterizes defensiveness.

Defensiveness stems from insecurity and has a potent effect on later learning. It is earmarked by the repeated use of modes of thought that were learned in the past and that can be expected to maintain predictability when applied to a current problem. Remediation through therapy requires that the individual learn alternatives to substitute for his defensive modes of thought. The learning of alternatives is engendered somewhat by the variable demands of the individual's desires and the environment and his desire to improve prediction. However, the effective deliberation and use of alternatives is much more dependent upon the teaching of such subjects as logic, math, and science than it is upon accidental learning. In both education and therapy the individual must improve his ability to predict by learning additional ideas that will promote accurate predictions and by learning to deliberate effectively.

The same environmental arrangement is appropriate for both therapy and education—that is, it should help to validate desirable predictions and should never issue punitive feedback.

Therapy is a much more difficult kind of teaching than education because the individual undergoing therapy is insecure; he tends to retain defensive modes in order to maintain predictability and he is less likely to consider unfamiliar alternatives. Furthermore, in therapy, inaccurate predictions must be unlearned while accurate predictions are being learned. As in education, the environment provided should confirm the desired prediction or otherwise be irrelevant, to prevent mislearning. But in addition, environmental cues should not be allowed to confirm the undesirable prediction, so that it may be extinguished. The person in therapy should be led to believe that environmental demands call only for the confirmation of the desired predictions and are never punitive, and that the undesirable predictions are not relevant to the situation and are therefore maladaptive.

A similar arrangement of the environment is claimed for the procedures used during brainwashing to change behavior, although our knowledge of the process is quite limited. The subject is never punished, but he is placed in a topsy-turvy world in which none of the predictions he is accustomed to making are validated. However secure he may have been in the past, he soon becomes very insecure. He becomes desperate to establish a predictable relationship with the environment once again. The only way that he can re-establish predictability is to formulate predictions the environment will confirm.

His instructors arrange the environment so that only certain predetermined predictions are confirmed. These predictions are based upon the values of the social group into which his instructors are attempting to indoctrinate him. Holding him in the helpless state of unpredictability, they encourage him to try their way of behaving, suggesting that he need only adjust to the inevitability of the demands of the environment in which he finds himself, as anyone must, in order to establish a predictable relationship with his new environment.

They claim that they are not punishing him, even challenging him to cite one instance in which they actively attempted to harm him. They suggest that they are asking him to conform to the same environmental demands to which they themselves must conform, and they offer to help him adjust. Placing him in an unpredictable environment, they offer to teach him how to predict and control himself in his new surroundings. The claim is that the subject succumbs to the conversion. He enters brainwashing with one set of values and predictions, and emerges with another. He relinquishes the predictions he learned from his former reference group and learns the predictions that emanate from the social values of the group into which he is being indoctrinated.

Bettelheim's account of his experiences in a concentration camp illustrates such a struggle to maintain predictability. He writes: "Besides traumatization the Gestapo relied mainly on three other methods of destroying all personal autonomy. The first was that of forcing prisoners to adopt childlike behavior. The second was that of forcing them to give up individuality and merge them into an amorphous mass. The third consisted of destroying all capacity for self-determination, all ability to predict the future and thus to prepare for it. . . . By destroying man's ability to act on his own or to predict the outcome of his own actions, they destroyed the feeling that his actions had any purpose."[2] With regard to his own frame of mind, Bettelheim states: "What had most value for me was that things happened according to expectation; that therefore my future in the camp was at least partly predictable from what I was already experiencing and from what I had read."[3]

However, there is a substantial difference between brainwashing and the methods used in the Nazi concentration camps in that punishment was also inflicted to help destroy the individual's ability to predict, whereas during brainwashing great care is taken not to coerce the prisoner. My theory explains why brainwashing should be the more successful method of converting the values and expectations of the individual.

As in brainwashing, therapy should involve an intentional arrangement of the environment, whether the sessions are held with a group or between a single psychotherapist and his patient, and whether the conversations last only an hour or for twenty-four hours in a controlled setting. The problem in conducting therapy in the same environment that engendered hostility in the indi-

[2] Bruno Bettelheim, *The Informed Heart*, pp. 131, 148.
[3] Ibid., p. 126.

vidual in the first place is that the environment may continue to confirm the predictions that engendered the hostility, making it difficult to extinguish these predictions. It therefore seems advisable to change the milieu of the individual in order to conduct effective therapy.

AFTERWORD

In this book I have attempted to address the problem of behavior from a different vantage point, focusing on the influence of rationality and higher mental functions. The foundation for this theoretical perspective is the assumption that a primary motive of the individual is to predict his relationship with his environment. His mental operations and actions function to fulfill this motive.

I have described the different modes of thought and have noted that the deliberation of abstractions is the mode through which the individual attains excellence, the apex of which is the discovery of something new to all men. I have also discussed the importance of society in promoting the development of prediction and control.

The theory I have proposed in this volume not only is consistent with the results of much of the research that has been accumulated over the years but also appears to integrate these results within a distinct conceptual framework that permits the behavior of individuals to be viewed as one determined by mental process.

I hope that this theory will stimulate others to constructive thought about the puzzling behavior of individuals and that the explanations I have offered will assist in penetrating some of the mysteries of the mind. Perhaps it will contribute to the development of a psychological approach to human behavior, an approach that might be called rational psychology.

176

Afterword

Research is being conducted by me and others to determine the relationship between a person's predictive ability and his success in many areas of life—for instance, in earning money or achieving social status or having unusual ability to solve problems. I have devised a test to measure predictive ability in individuals. A person's rating on such a test can be compared with his I.Q. to determine the relative importance of predictive ability and intelligence in contributing to his success or failure in various fields of endeavor. Since the test also measures an individual's confidence in his ability to predict, it can also be used to determine how his degree of confidence is related to his personal adjustment.

Even the motive to predict can itself be compared with other motives to determine the relative importance of each in directing behavior. (Some of the other motives were discussed in chapter 3.)

Many of the hypotheses to be derived from the theory concern mental operations. The testing of these will involve instruments that can be used to observe and measure brain function. Great strides have been made in recent years in the development of highly sophisticated instruments and techniques for use in brain research, and it is likely that progress will continue in this field.

There are many testable hypotheses to be derived from the theory. Some of these hypotheses are the following:

• When a person believes he is failing to maintain a predictable relationship with the environment, he will attempt to ensure predictability at the expense of pursuing his preferences and attempting to predict unfamiliar stimuli.

• Conversely, when he is confident that he is maintaining a predictable relationship with the environment, he will attempt to pursue his preferences and predict unfamiliar stimuli to extend his scope of prediction.

• An individual may be aware of the intensity of his feelings without being aware of the content of the event associated with his feelings; but if he is aware of the content of an event, he will also be aware of the feelings he associates with the event.

• An excessive intensity of feeling, whether positive or negative, interferes with one's ability to predict accurately.

• A person who can predict the pleasure he wishes to obtain can tolerate its delay better than one who is uncertain whether he will be able to acquire the pleasure he wishes to obtain.

• When a source of pleasure is available, but not predictable, the individual will tend to overindulge himself.

• Self-confidence, self-respect, and personal security are positively correlated with each other and the ability to predict accurately.

• When an individual conceives of a way to predict a previously unpredictable stimulation associated with high arousal, he will attempt to confirm the prediction.

• A person who lacks self-confidence will avoid predicting the unfamiliar and resort to defensiveness more often than will a self-confident individual.

• When a person is aware of the implications for prediction of the material he is to learn, he will be more motivated to learn the material.

There are several other similar hypotheses stated in chapter 13, concerning the way in which the environment may be arranged to facilitate prediction. However, it is my purpose here not to make an exhaustive list of such hypotheses but simply to indicate how the theory I have put forth may be tested and applied.

BIBLIOGRAPHY

Allport, Gordon W. *Becoming: Basic Considerations for a Psychology of Personality*. New Haven: Yale University Press, 1955.

Bartlett, Frederic. *Thinking: An Experimental and Social Study*. New York: Basic Books, 1958.

Berlyne, D. E. "Recent Developments in Piaget's Work." *British Journal of Educational Psychology* 27 (1957):1–12.

Bettelheim, Bruno. "Dialogue with Mothers." *Ladies' Home Journal*, December 1971, pp. 14, 16.

———. *The Informed Heart*. New York: Avon Books, 1960.

Bindra, Dalbir. *Motivation*. New York: Ronald Press, 1959.

Blau, Peter M. *Exchange and Power in Social Life*. New York: John Wiley & Sons, 1964.

Bolles, Robert C. "Reinforcement, Expectancy and Learning." *Psychological Review* 79 (1972):394–409.

Bruner, Jerome S., and Krech, David, eds. *Perception and Personality*. New York: Greenwood Press, 1968.

Bruner, Jerome S.; Goodnow, Jacqueline J.; and Austin, George A. *A Study of Thinking*. New York: John Wiley & Sons, 1956.

Carnap, Rudolf. *Meaning and Necessity: A Study in Semantics and Modal Logic*. Chicago: University of Chicago Press, 1956.

Dewey, John. *How We Think*. Boston: D. C. Heath, 1933.

BIBLIOGRAPHY

Estes, William K. "An Experimental Study of Punishment." No. 263 in *Psychological Monographs*, Vol. 57 (1944).

———. "Reinforcement in Human Behavior." *American Scientist* 60 (1972):723–29.

———. "The Statistical Approach to Learning Theory." In *Psychology: A Study of a Science*, edited by Sigmund Koch, pp. 380–491. New York: McGraw-Hill, 1959.

Freud, Sigmund. *The Ego and the Id*. London: Hogarth Press, 1950.

Fromm, Erich. *Escape from Freedom*. New York: Avon Books, 1971.

Gagné, Robert T. *The Conditions of Learning*. New York: Holt, Rinehart and Winston, Inc., 1965.

Galanter, Eugene, and Gerstenhaber, Murray. "On Thought: The Extrinsic Theory." *Psychological Review* 63 (1956):218–27.

Getzels, Jacob W., and Jackson, Philip W. *Creativity and Intelligence: Explorations with Gifted Students*. New York: John Wiley & Sons, 1962.

Haider, Manfred; Spong, Paul; and Lindsley, Donald B. "Attention, Vigilance and Cortical Evoked Potential in Humans." *Science* 145 (1964):180–82.

Hebb, Donald O. *The Organization of Behavior*. New York: John Wiley & Sons, 1949.

Hilgard, Ernest R. *Theories of Learning*. 1st ed. New York: Appleton-Century-Crofts, 1948. 2nd ed. New York: Appleton-Century-Crofts, 1956.

Homans, George C. *Social Behavior*. Edited by Robert K. Merton. New York: Harcourt, Brace, World, 1961.

Hull, Clark L. *A Behavior System*. New Haven, Conn.: Yale University Press, 1952.

Inhelder, Baerbal, and Piaget, Jean. *The Growth of Logical Thinking from Childhood to Adolescence*. New York: Basic Books, 1958.

BIBLIOGRAPHY

Johnson, Donald M. *The Psychology of Thought and Judgment.* New York: Harper & Row, 1955.

Jung, Carl. *The Undiscovered Self.* Boston: Little, Brown, 1957.

Kelly, George A. *The Psychology of Personal Constructs.* Vol. 1. New York: W. W. Norton, 1955.

Köhler, Wolfgang. "Physical Gestalten." In *A Source Book of Gestalt Psychology,* edited by Willis D. Ellis, pp. 17–54. New York: Harcourt, Brace, 1938.

Lewin, Kurt. *Field Theory in Social Science.* Edited by Dorwin Cartwright. New York: Harper & Row, 1951.

Lindmann, E. "Gamma Movement." In *A Source Book of Gestalt Psychology,* edited by Willis D. Ellis, pp. 173–81. New York: Harcourt, Brace, 1938.

London, Harvey, and Schubert, Daniel S. P. "Increase of Autonomic Arousal by Boredom." *Journal of Abnormal Psychology* 80 (1972):29–36.

Malmo, Robert B. "Activation: A Neuropsychological Dimension." *Psychological Review* 66 (1959):367–86.

Maslow, Abraham H. *Motivation and Personality.* New York: Harper & Row, 1954.

McKay, D. M. "Cerebral Organization and the Conscious Control of Action." In *Brain and Conscious Experience,* edited by John C. Eccles, pp. 422–45. New York: Springer, 1966.

Mead, George H. *Mind, Self, and Society.* Chicago: University of Chicago Press, 1934.

Menninger, Karl. *The Human Mind.* New York: Alfred A. Knopf, 1945.

Miller, George A.; Galanter, Eugene; and Pribram, Karl H. *Plans and the Structure of Behavior.* New York: Holt, Rinehart and Winston, 1960.

Mittlestaedt, H. "Experience and Capacity." In *Fourth Conference on Learning, Remembering and Forgetting,* edited by Daniel P. Kimble. Washington, D.C.: New York Academy of Sciences, Interdisciplinary Communications Program, 1968.

Mowrer, Orval H. *Learning Theory and the Symbolic Process.* New York: John Wiley & Sons, 1960.

Muenzinger, Karl F. *Reward and Punishment.* University of Colorado Studies, General Series (A), Vol. 27 (December 1946).

———, and Gentry, Evelyn. "Tone Discrimination in White Rats." *Journal of Comparative Psychology* 12 (1931):195–206.

Newell, Allen, and Shaw, John C. "Programming the Logic Theory Machine." *Proceedings of the Joint Computer Conference, Los Angeles,* February 1957, pp. 230–40.

Newell, Allen; Shaw, John C.; and Simon, Herbert A. "Elements of a Theory of Human Problem Solving." *Psychological Review* 65 (1958):151–66.

Newell, Allen, and Simon, Herbert A. "The Logic Machine: A Complex Information Processing System." In *IEEE* [*Institute of Electrical and Electronics Engineers*] *Transactions on Information Theory,* edited by Joseph E. Rowe. Vol. IT-2 (3) (1956):61–79.

Osgood, Charles E.; Suci, George J.; and Tannenbaum, Percy H. *The Measurement of Meaning.* Urbana: University of Illinois Press, 1957.

Parsons, Talcott. *Social Structure and Personality.* New York: Free Press of Glencoe, 1964.

———. *The Social System.* Glencoe, Ill.: Free Press, 1951.

Piaget, Jean. *Logic and Psychology.* New York: Basic Books, 1957.

———. *The Origins of Intelligence in Children.* New York: W. W. Norton, 1963.

———, and Szeminski, A. *The Child's Conception of Numbers* (1941), translated by C. Gattegno and F. M. Hodgson. New York: Humanities Press, 1952.

Pribram, Karl H. "Emotion: Steps toward a Neuropsychological Theory." In *Neurophysiology and Emotion,* edited by David C.

BIBLIOGRAPHY

Glass, pp. 3–40. New York: Rockefeller University Press and Russell Sage Foundation, 1967.

Skinner, B. F. *Verbal Behavior*. New York: Appleton-Century-Crofts, 1957.

———. "What Is the Experimental Analysis of Behavior?" *Journal of the Experimental Analysis of Behavior* 9 (1966):213–18.

Sokolov, E. N. "Neuronal Models and the Orienting Reflex." In *The Central Nervous System and Behavior*, edited by Mary A. B. Brazier, vol. 3. New York: Josiah Macy, Jr., Foundation, 1960.

Spence, Kenneth W. *Behavior Theory and Learning: Selected Papers*. Englewood Cliffs, N.J.: Prentice-Hall, 1960.

Sutton, Samuel; Tueting, Patricia; and John, E. R. "Information Delivery and the Sensory Evoked Potential." *Science* 155 (1967):1426–39.

Teuber, H. L. "Perception." In *Handbook of Physiology*. Vol. 3: *Neurophysiology*, edited by John Field, H. W. Magaeen, and V. E. Hall, pp. 1595–1668. Washington: American Psychological Society, 1960.

Thorndike, Edward L. "Reward and Punishment in Animal Learning." *Comparative Psychological Monographs* 8 (1932): 1–65.

Tolman, Edward C. *Collected Papers in Psychology*. Berkeley: University of California Press, 1951.

———. "Principles of Purposive Behavior." In *Psychology: A Study of a Science*, edited by Sigmund Koch, Vol. 2, pp. 92–157. New York: McGraw-Hill, 1959.

———. *Purposive Behavior in Animals and Men*. New York: Appleton-Century-Crofts, 1932.

Travers, Robert M. W. *Essentials of Learning*. New York: Macmillan, 1963.

Walter, W. Gray. "Slow Potential Waves in Human Brain Associated with Expectancy, Attention and Decision." *Archiv für*

BIBLIOGRAPHY

Psychiatrie und Zeitschrift, f. d. ges, Neurologie 206 (1964: 309–22.

Wertheimer, Max. "Laws of Organization in Perceptual Forms." In *A Source Book of Gestalt Psychology*, edited by Willis D. Ellis, pp. 71–88. New York: Harcourt, Brace, 1938.

White, Robert W. "Motivation Reconsidered: The Concept of Competence." *Psychological Review* 66 (1959):297–333.

Wulf, Friedrich. "Tendencies in Figural Variation." In *A Source Book of Gestalt Psychology*, edited by Willis D. Ellis, pp. 136–48. New York: Harcourt, Brace, 1938.

INDEX

185

Rational Behavior

Composed in Linotype Electra by Kingsport Press, Inc., with selected lines of display in Monotype Deepdene.

Printed letterpress by Kingsport Press on Warren's University Text, an acid-free paper noted for its longevity. The paper was expressly watermarked for the University of South Carolina Press with the Press colophon.

Binding by Kingsport Press in Balacron 2200 Linen.

Designed by Robert L. Nance.